How to Keep Going When the Storms Keep Coming

ROSS CAMPBELL
with RANDALL GRAY

Tyndale House Publishers, Inc.
Wheaton, Illinois

Scripture quotations are taken from The Holy Bible,
King James Version, *The Living Bible*, and the *New
American Standard Bible* (© The Lockman
Foundation, 1960, 1962, 1963, 1968, 1971).

Cover photo © The Image Bank/L. D. Gordon

First printing, November 1986
Library of Congress Catalog Card Number 86-50650
ISBN 0-8423-1376-1
Copyright © 1986 by Ross Campbell
Printed in the United States of America

To P A T
whose strength
tolerance
and
understanding
have made
this book
possible

ow blessed is the man who does not walk in the counsel of the wicked, nor stand in the path of sinners, nor sit in the seat of scoffers!

*But his delight is in the law of the L*ORD, *and in His law he meditates day and night.*

And he will be like a tree firmly planted by streams of water, which yields its fruit in its season, and its leaf does not wither; and in whatever he does, he prospers (Ps. 1:1-3, NASB).

CONTENTS

ACKNOWLEDGMENTS

This book is a culmination of many years of living and
the influence of numerous people whose lives have
intersected with mine. Identifying each individual by
name and acknowledging his or her specific contribution
to my life would be an exhausting, if not futile, exercise.
I'd be bound to forget someone. So I'll simply say thanks
to these people, some of whom are mentioned in the
following pages.

I am also grateful to Dr. John Baucom, a trusted
associate of mine, for reading portions of the manuscript
and offering valuable responses. His suggestions have
truly helped give the book an extra dimension.

Second, I wish to express gratitude to my pastor,
Monty Jordan, whose generous, loving spirit and insights
on life have served as the bases for many of the book's
strongest points. Spiritual perspective is made possible

through the example and counsel of people like him and his fine family.

Deep thanks is due to Jim Hefley—a fine writer in his own right—for his expert editing skills and the continued support and encouragement he and his wife Marty have offered during the book's writing.

A very special acknowledgment is made to Randall Gray for making a remarkable transformation from newspaper editor and reporter to my collaborative assistant on this project. His sparkling creativity and commitment to excellence have shaped the work into more than I ever hoped it could be.

And finally, to the loves of my life—Pat, Carey, Cathy, David, Dale, Chris, and the rest of my family—my wholehearted appreciation. The support, love, and downright courage they repeatedly display have made our family a solid tree with deep roots, which, I believe. no storm can disturb.

PROLOGUE

It took several rings of the telephone before I realized the sound of jangling bells was not a part of my dreams. While I groped in the darkness for the phone, I glanced at our bedside digital clock. The lit numerals read 12:06. After fumbling momentarily with the receiver, I answered with a groggy hello.

"Ross, this is John," came the urgent voice of one of my associates. "Listen, I'm on call tonight, and I really hate to disturb you, but Carl Wallace jumped off the Market Street Bridge tonight. They pronounced him dead shortly after 11:30."

A shudder ran through me as I sat up, now wide awake. "Oh, John," I moaned. "I'm sorry to hear it. Are you going to follow up?"

"Yeah, yeah," he said quietly. "I thought I'd head over to the hospital and meet with the family."

"OK, that's good. Call me back if I can be of help."

My eyes had become accustomed to the darkness, and our bedroom, bathed in the pale light of a full moon, suddenly seemed brighter. "What's wrong?" Pat said, rolling toward me.

"We've got a problem," I answered. "A suicide."

Falling immediately back to sleep would be out of the question, so I threw on my bathrobe and headed to the kitchen for some milk.

After a glass of milk and thirty minutes of television, I still wasn't drowsy. I cut off the set and flopped down on the couch anyway. "I've got to get some sleep," I muttered.

When 6:30 A.M. rolled around I had slept very little. Wearily, I headed upstairs to get dressed.

At work, I fought off my fatigue as best as I could and received the usual stream of Tuesday morning patients. By midmorning I was somewhat more alert, but I still couldn't purge myself of remorse over the bad news I heard the night before.

I couldn't have been in a worse frame of mind when more crushing news came to the office. A young husband and father, a member of the Sunday school class I taught, had just been found dead. He'd apparently taken his own life, too. Another suicide!

The report absolutely floored me. This young man had been struggling through some problems, but they hadn't seemed insurmountable. He'd always had a ready smile and a positive outlook toward the future. I somehow stumbled through the rest of the day, dazed by the incredible events of the past eighteen hours.

On my way home from the hospital that evening, I decided to check back at the office. Through the phone in my car, I learned that several of my associates were absolutely taxed to the limit with emergency appointments. John had spent much of the day at a local high school, counseling the school faculty in the aftermath of two student suicides during a three-week period. Besides this, local psychiatric hospitals were practically filled to capacity.

What is going on? I thought in disbelief, after hanging up. *Why can't these people be helped? What more can we do?*

At home, Pat expressed concern over my state of mind. This sudden cluster of suicides had indeed fueled my own feelings of hopelessness.

"What's for dinner?" I asked as I slumped down in my favorite chair. "But then, it doesn't matter. I can't eat a thing."

The week had barely begun, but the shocking events of the past two days seemed to have taken a month's toll on me.

I was tempted to resent my profession and its often concealed pressures. But after a time my head cleared, and I began trying to understand the emotional turmoil gripping my community—and more specifically, two seemingly healthy individuals.

What these two men had needed—and what their families no doubt were desperately seeking now—was a sense of hope. Certainly, that's what all of us constantly seek in our lives.

It's been my experience that hope, or spiritual perspective in the midst of crisis, doesn't simply happen with the passing of time. Only when others are willing to actively assist hurting people put their lives back into proper perspective does hope return and blossom.

Through my office door come individuals churning with emotional turmoil and beset by depression, fear, anger, guilt, and frustration. Many of them are professing Christians, some are Jewish, a few claim no spiritual faith. The believers tend to be doubly distressed because they think, and perhaps were taught, that faith in God helps one sail through life on a flowery bed of ease. They forget the biblical prediction, "In the world ye shall have tribulation . . ." (John 16:33, KJV).

They're desperately trying to keep their heads above water while they feel their ship sinking underneath them. But the emotional trauma is so great for many of them that they dread even getting out of bed in the morning. The lack of perspective that can occur when they are in the throes of a guilt- or fear-producing crisis impedes their ability to remain afloat emotionally and spiritually.

I know. I've shared the same sinking feeling many times.

The first few years after my commitment to Christ I had no difficulty maintaining my spiritual perspective. Everything was new and exciting, and the smooth path before me seemed to stretch on forever. Then the first big storm came (chapter 2) and almost wiped me out.

After that, the storms kept coming, even as severe weather keeps rolling across the country during a really bad winter or spring. The stormy season of my soul lasted more than fifteen years. I bounced up and down in frightening turbulence while attempting to fly spiritually by the seat of my pants. But I would gain spiritual perspective only to lose it in the next crisis and become once again confused, disheartened, pessimistic—even angry at God.

Like Peter on the Sea of Galilee, I would take my eyes off Jesus and focus on the wind and waves. Afraid and beginning to sink, I cried so many times, as did the fisherman apostle, "Lord, help me!" And always, when I looked up, I saw Jesus' outstretched hand.

There were times when I hesitated. Held back by doubts and sometimes pride, I just caused myself more misery. It was only when I said, "Lord, I'm trusting you to give me perspective," and took hold of his hand, that the storm would begin to subside. My frustration eased, my anger cooled, my disposition improved when I reached out to the One who stilled not only the raging elements but also the tempests in men's souls.

What I needed when I was caught in the middle-years' trap, as I've termed it, was counsel and companionship from older, more mature believers who had crossed the deep valleys of life before me. I simply didn't have at the time a storehouse of past experiences upon which to draw that demonstrated God's abiding grace. I combed libraries and bookstores for biographies and found little help. It appears the biographers or the publishers weed out the problems and doubts from the lives of great saints.

For a stumbler like me, this only made life worse. I imagined truly dedicated Christians didn't experience troubles and heart searchings like mine.

Since emerging from my days in the "slough of despond," I've observed other Christians making the same mistakes I did. Sometimes it has been terribly hard, if not impractical, for a churchman, a father, a doctor, a medical missionary, and now a psychiatrist to admit that he has made blunders like those who look to him for guidance. Some people need to see a counselor as someone who lives above crises and problems; others are quick to criticize admissions of failure.

But finally, I decided to put my deep valleys in a book, in hopes of helping others avoid the same pitfalls I have faced. If I had had such a book from a veteran, I believe I would have been spared an ocean of emotional pain.

A word about the format: This is not an autobiography. Nor is it a self-help manual, similar to my earlier books, *How to Really Love Your Child* and *How to Really Love Your Teenager* (both by Victor Books). Rather, this is a compilation of stories that show how after much stumbling, I found spiritual perspective in the midst of crisis.

The episodes are as intensely autobiographical as they are varied. (I've always believed the Lord was preparing me for the field of psychiatry through a diversity of tribulations.) Each story stands on its own, giving a

different insight. I have changed the names of many
people and places, but the dialogue and events have
been reconstructed to the best of my recollection.

My hope is that the stories will be universal enough
to help you see the guiding light beyond your own
deep valleys and rough waters. I also hope you'll laugh
out loud if any of my foibles or those of the other
characters amuse you. Laughter is still a marvelous tonic.

I pray that as I relate the struggles of my pilgrimage,
your voyage will be made smoother and your spiritual
perspective will become clearer. If the book merely
provokes you to think about how your own perspective
might be improved, then I've succeeded. Should these
stories move you to reach out to a friend in need, then
all the better.

CHAPTER

MY FIRST ENCOUNTER

The old Girl Scout retreat facility looked plain and uninviting. Recently converted into a navy lodge, the weathered structure of stone and wood stood starkly against a backdrop of drab woodland. Officially, it was springtime, but the unseasonably cool weather in this section of southeastern Pennsylvania had stifled the characteristic budding of the trees. I could understand the buds' reluctance to expose themselves to these conditions; I had on my midshipman's woolen winter uniform, and I was still cold.

Our busload of midshipmen had ridden in silence for most of the two-hundred-mile trip from Annapolis to Willow Grove, Pennsylvania, for the Officers' Christian Fellowship (OCF) Spring Leave Conference. Save for a few occasional snores of schoolmates catching up on their sleep, only the steady whine of our bus's engine pierced the quiet. I was too numbed by the lingering winter weather and the just-completed scramble to turn in assignments to doze off.

Now, however, as we neared our destination, my fellow riders began coming to life.

"How's it feel to have survived another semester?" someone shouted. Cheers erupted. "You're sure you passed?" another answered back. "I read that English term paper you turned in. Pretty shabby stuff." I joined in the uproarious laughter that filled the bus.

As we bounced along the rutted road leading to the lodge, I felt myself caught up in the radiant spirit of togetherness that burned among this group of midshipmen. My lowly status as a first-year plebe at the U.S. Naval Academy posed no obstacle to acceptance into this newfound fellowship composed largely of upper-classmen. Their zestfulness and ability to turn a shoulder to the grind of everyday life—especially noticeable among the senior leaders—had drawn me to OCF and the annual Spring Leave Conference.

Something new bubbled up in me. Though outwardly winter's gloom prevailed, within I experienced a warmth—a feeling of belonging. I, Ross Campbell, an eighteen-year-old plebe whose home was thousands of miles away in New Mexico, belonged to this group of strangers, diverse in backgrounds, but bound by their . . .

Bound by what? I deliberated. *Camaraderie? Joy? Their Christianity? Is it the knowledge that Jesus Christ was a good man—a man whose life is worth emulating—that produces the bond among these men? Or is it more?*

I puzzled over the positive emotion demonstrated by my peers. I recalled seeing the same exuberance during city-wide youth hymn sings in Albuquerque. I had served as president of this annual youth event one year, and had noticed the contentment among the members of certain denominations in particular. I knew then, as I know now, that Jesus was supposed to have been a positive social force in his day, but how did that fact translate into all this joy? *Either I must be very naive,* I thought, *or these people are just very easy to get along with.*

Larry Ingles, a bubbly, well-liked second classman (junior), had invited me to attend the Spring Leave Conference as an alternative to spending four days galavanting in town, as many of my classmates planned to do. The conference seemed a good enough way to kill four days. As it was, I had neither the money for the bus ticket nor a sufficient amount of leave time to make the trip home to Albuquerque.

Larry had introduced himself to me at a Bible study in the Bancroft Hall dormitory on campus. I had sought out the study after dinner one evening looking for companionship. He shared some Scriptures with me and introduced me to some of his friends. They all had that same look of contentment on their faces. It was as if they'd discovered a cure for disease or something.

I agreed to go to the Spring Leave Conference primarily because I had nothing better to do, but also because my curiosity had been piqued. Members of the OCF in Bancroft Hall knew something and felt something that I didn't. I wanted to discover what it was.

As our bus squealed to a halt, I noticed that none of my comrades looked upon the old two-story, log-built lodge with the same disdain and disappointment as I did. The fact that many of these men had attended previous OCF spring conferences, and now looked forward to this one, gave me encouragement. Maybe I was where I ought to be. My cold feet, hands, and nose, however, told me otherwise.

A cruel blast of wind slammed into us as we filed off the bus. Subfreezing gusts of air whipped at the baggy pant legs of our uniforms and played havoc with the caps atop our heads. I turned up the collar of my pea coat and dipped my head to brace against the wind.

I hated this weather. The darkening sky and grayish thicket of surrounding trees added to my misery. But these OCF guys! They continued talking animatedly, oblivious, it seemed, to the same early night air that had me shivering.

Why are these guys so happy all the time? I wondered. *How do they meet everything with such . . . joy?*

We assembled on the front porch of the lodge. In a moment, out came a young ensign whose job it was to escort us to our rooms. His cheeks were red from the cold, but his face bore a cheerful smile.

"Evening, gentlemen," he said. "Cold enough for you? It's good and warm in here," he commented, reaching for the handle of the front door.

He's got it, too, I thought. *That same glow . . .*

Through the large, front windows I could see a host of people, including army and navy officers, their wives, and several casually dressed civilians. They stood drinking coffee before a huge fireplace with an inviting blaze. Long flickering shadows danced high upon the great room's rustic walls to the beamed ceiling. Above the stone-hewn mantel hung several naval banners. In the center of the wall was a portrait of Jesus.

"Look at all that brass," quipped one of the group as we were led past high-ranking officers, including admirals and generals, to the stairway. "It sure shines nice," chimed another.

The warmth emanating from the fire had reached us as soon as we entered the lodge. I wanted to join the impressive-looking group and share a cup of coffee.

"I didn't expect anything like this," I commented to the midshipman standing next to me. My voice was tinged with awe. The fellow in earshot of my statement turned and smiled.

I felt a little embarrassed, but I knew each man in the group was equally impressed by the high-ranking military officials assembled in the room. The prospect of rubbing elbows with admirals, generals, colonels—even the commander of the Caribbean fleet—would have been heady even if I hadn't been enrolled at Annapolis.

"Find yourselves an empty bunk and get ready for dinner," the ensign instructed from the top of the stairs. "Dinner's at 1830. We're glad you people could make it."

After locating an empty room and freshening up, I joined my bus mates out in the hall. We had agreed to eat dinner as a group.

During the meal we learned the agenda of speakers for the conference. The first speaker to be introduced was Dr. Bob Smith, a lean, tall man wearing glasses. His gentle, compassionate voice matched his unassuming, somewhat frail appearance. He had been a pastor, but now he served as professor of philosophy at Bethel College in St. Paul, Minnesota.

Next was Cleo Buxton, the executive director of OCF. A former U.S. Army captain during World War II, he had discovered the OCF (then the Officers' Christian Union) when recalled to active duty during the Korean conflict and became the first staff member of the American OCU in 1952. His forceful manner of speaking immediately commanded my attention. I could understand why this rugged man who spoke with such conviction and clarity was so greatly admired within the military.

With the initial conference business having been attended to, the remainder of the evening was devoted to a rousing time of hymn singing and prayer.

"Then sings my soul, my Savior God to Thee . . . ," I sang in unison with the gathering of men and women. The robust strains of the hymn gave me gooseflesh. "Onward, Christian Soldiers," with its stirring marching

cadence, provided an appropriate finale to the meeting. I
went off to bed humming the melodies of old hymns I
thought I'd forgotten.

Just before lying down to sleep, I went to my door and
peeked out. The lights remained on in most of the
rooms. In the one diagonally to my right, I saw a young
ensign kneeling beside his bed in prayer. To my left, an
army colonel and a navy captain were reading the Bible
together. I felt guilty for intruding on these very private
scenes, but I stood there momentarily, leaning against the
doorway and trying to assimilate all I had experienced
that day.

*What is it that commands all this devotion among
all these men to a Man they've never met?* I walked to
my bed and knelt beside it. I felt awkward not knowing
what I wanted to say. "God, take care of my family," I
whispered finally.

I crawled into bed, pulling the cold sheets up over
me. "And show me what I need to know about you," I
added.

With some regret I concluded that the only real insight
I had into the Christian faith I had gained on my own.
The earliest recollection of my efforts to understand this
vast, mysterious force called God, I realized, hearkened
back to when I was a sixteen-year-old.

I would take the little free time I had from school and
my paper route to drive my '53 Chevrolet into the New
Mexico desert alone. Parked on a flat stretch of ground
that rose far away into the hazy Rocky Mountains, I
would read the Sunday paper and listen to preachers on
the radio, especially my favorite, M. R. DeHaan, M.D.

I cherished these private moments as I sought to come
to grips with the world and its strife, on the one hand,
and the radio's promise of freedom from fear, loneliness,
and guilt on the other.

Even then, alone in the majestic, still setting, I had
pieced together a prayer that God would help me make

some sense out of life, help me know where Donald
Ross Campbell fit into this big, big world.

My thoughts came back to the present. *My prayers
haven't developed very far, God. You'll have to teach
me what to say.*

Good food and companionship at breakfast the following
morning made me forget the prayer I had prayed the
night before. As Cleo Buxton began to speak, however, I
recalled my simple request and reexperienced the
yearning in my heart. *There has to be something more
than I already know,* I reflected.

"Without a personal relationship with Jesus Christ,"
Cleo boomed, "your life is a mockery. It's counterfeit.
But when you come to know Jesus personally, when you
walk and talk with him daily, your make-believe
happiness becomes real beyond your imagination.

"To know Jesus is to know the fullness of life and love
that God has promised you."

With each powerful phrase spoken by this barrel-
chested, deep-voiced army veteran, a new awareness
sprang up in me. It was one of those moments of shining
insight when it seemed as if the pieces of a complex
puzzle began to tumble into place.

"Jesus was not some ancient figure who left a legacy of
teachings for good people to follow," Cleo continued.
"He is alive right now. He is available to help you with
your life."

This transforming knowledge was almost more than I
could hold. Deeply moved, I asked Jesus right then to
make his life, love, and power known to me. I wanted
the joy and peace that was reflected in the lives and
faces of my Christian classmates.

All that day and before I fell asleep that night, the
word *mockery* spun in my thoughts. Had my life been
a mockery? Was it less than it ought to be? And was Jesus
what I needed to fill my yearning for meaning and

purpose? The answer to each of those questions was undeniably yes.

During the remainder of the conference, I soaked up every word delivered by the two featured speakers. Their talks reminded me of conversations I had had with Jim Wilson, the campus director of Officers' Christian Fellowship and the manager of an off-campus Christian bookstore, who I had come to know prior to the conference. Jim had graduated from the naval academy in 1950 and felt led by God to return to Annapolis to assist the midshipmen in OCF. His easy smile and caring disposition made me feel good just to be around him. And now his personal witness was something I was coming to identify with. I could hardly wait to share my decision with Jim.

In my room the night before our departure, I concluded I would profess my new relationship with Jesus Christ after I returned to campus. I knew I couldn't pick a better place to do so than at the U.S. Naval Academy, where there was already such a solid base of Christians.

On the bus trip back, my countenance of joy probably matched those of my Christian classmates. Nothing regarding my outward appearance concerned me, however. It was the thrilling inner warmth I felt that mattered. I couldn't wait to show it, to speak it, to live it: Jesus Christ was alive in me!

The spring chill that greeted us in Willow Grove and chased our bus back to Annapolis left its mark on me in the form of a cold. By the time we returned, I felt miserable. I had anticipated "coming down from the mountaintop" eventually, but I hadn't expected to hit bottom so hard.

It was about 1530 (3:30 P.M.) on the final day of spring leave when I got back to my room. The midshipmen who'd managed to get home for a few days would be arriving during the afternoon and night.

Sneezing and shivering in my rack, I wasn't up to the typically boisterous influx of returning classmates. And I certainly wasn't ready to commence with the hectic schedule of classes.

My watery eyes had just closed when the call came echoing down the hallway. "Campbell! Ross Campbell. Telephone."

Throwing on my robe and slippers, I stumbled down the hall to grab the receiver. Doug Graham's voice was on the line. Doug was a former naval officer who supported OCF, and I had talked briefly with him at the conference.

"You don't sound too good, Ross," he said. "You sick?"

"Yeah, it hit me a couple of hours ago. The lodge was a little drafty, wasn't it?"

Doug cackled with laughter. "Yeah, I guess it was. You should have slept by the fireplace. That's the only warm spot in the place.

"Listen, Ross. I'm calling for two reasons: One, to congratulate you on your decision, and two, to ask you to give your testimony at the next OCF meeting. It would be a great help to a lot of the guys who haven't been able to make a decision."

I was amazed that Doug had realized I'd accepted Christ. I turned my head to sneeze.

At a loss for words, I simply said, "When?"

"In two weeks, during the regular Bible study hour after dinner."

I sneezed again. "Well, I don't know," I said. "If you really want me to. You might have to coach me a little. Give me some pointers on what to say."

"Oh, you'll do fine," he replied. "I'll give you a book sometime next week that will help out. OK? Whaddya say?"

"Well, OK. If you insist. I'm flattered you should ask."

"Just don't croak between now and then," he laughed.

Back under the covers, I had second thoughts about agreeing to give a personal testimony. I wanted to share my newfound faith and put it into action on campus, but this was sooner than I'd expected.

Much to my delight, the same fervent mood that had been present during the conference continued on campus. After several days in the warm fellowship of my OCF buddies and steady dosages of aspirin, my spirits improved considerably.

The Bible studies at Bancroft Hall generated enormous enthusiasm in the aftermath of the conference. A packed room was on hand the night of my scheduled testimony. I was scared to death. Jim Wilson's presence at the meeting, however, put me a little more at ease.

I felt uncomfortable taking the leader's chair, which was situated behind a small desk in roughly the center of the floor. A large number of fellow midshipmen sprawled wherever they could find a space.

After opening with prayer, I asked the men to turn in their Bibles to Galatians 2:20. The brief lull permitted me to take a deep breath.

"I heard this Scripture during the recent OCF spring conference, where I made a decision to accept Christ," I said. "I thought I'd read it and just briefly tell what it means to me.

" 'I am crucified with Christ; nevertheless I live; yet not I, but Christ liveth in me: and the life which I now live in the flesh I live by the faith of the Son of God, who loved me, and gave himself for me.' "

I looked into the sea of faces, fighting to control my anxiety. "This pretty much says it all to me. The Scripture indicates that in becoming a Christian, each of us dies unto himself and becomes bound to Jesus. We're new creatures. Our old natures are cast aside."

It appeared that I had everyone's attention, so I went on. "This is what I sought to find when I went to the spring conference," I said. "I wanted to change for the better, and I wanted to know what it was about Jesus that made the OCF guys dedicate their lives to him.

"The Bible tells us what commands such devotion: love. The Son of God, God himself, loves us. And Jesus died to prove it to all men once and for all." I struggled to talk through the lump in my throat.

"And I just want everyone who doesn't know this, to know it and accept it. If you're not a Christian, I hope you'll consider becoming one."

When I was finished, everyone just sat still for a moment. I didn't know why for sure, but I sensed they were all as moved as I was. Jim winked at me when I asked him to close in prayer.

"Well done," Jim said after the meeting. "You're a natural, Ross. The Lord is going to use you here."

OCF's ongoing witness spread like wildfire. It was with a great deal of pride that we in the OCF viewed our accomplishments among the midshipmen at Bancroft Hall.

By my second year, "Mother Bancroft," as we called it, "the largest dormitory in the world" with six wings able to accommodate four thousand men, had become a center for serious religious thought and spiritual revival.

Different OCF members volunteered each week to conduct the Bible studies in their rooms. The locations changed, but the sight at each session was the same. Men dressed in their skivvies and bathrobes, often with towels draped around their necks and toothbrushes in their pockets, stood, lay across the bunks, or sat cross-legged on the floor as a fellow midshipman read and interpreted God's Word. Usually thirty to forty men attended each meeting, causing the impromptu assemblies to spill out into the hall.

Professions of faith were made at many meetings, and baptisms were conducted at surrounding churches. We had each other for support, and we listened eagerly to one another's joys and hurts. There was no reason, we said, that one should fall without the others sharing in the pain. There could not have been a more fertile ground for sowing the seeds of the gospel.

In my third year I was chosen by my Christian peers to direct the Naval Academy Christian Association, as well as the OCF. The honor of leading such fine groups of fellow Christians was tremendously gratifying. However, I derived my greatest satisfaction in seeing the eagerness with which the navy's future officers drank in the message of Jesus Christ as Savior.

As the memberships of the OCF and the NACA grew, so also did the demand for additional Bible study sessions. By my senior year, the OCF was asked to conduct more than the six Bible study sessions being held weekly in each of Bancroft Hall's respective wings. We already were holding regular OCF activities to supplement the Bible studies—the weekend and Spring Leave conferences, for example—but still the call went up for more.

Midshipmen came to know Jesus Christ by the scores at Bible study sessions and OCF conferences. I sincerely began to believe that the United States Naval Academy would come to produce more new Christians than any other institution in the world! I couldn't imagine anything that would derail the movement and dampen my enthusiasm. That was my first big mistake.

➡️*If any man be in Christ, he is a new creature* . . . (2 Cor. 5:17, KJV).

➡️ *What the sunshine is to the flower, the Lord Jesus Christ is to my soul* (Alfred Lord Tennyson).

CHAPTER

NAVY TRIALS

December was upon us at Annapolis, and the
anticipation of sharing Christmas with my family in New
Mexico was mounting. I was in my fourth year, and if
things continued to go well I would be commissioned an
ensign in the spring. I was excited that so many
midshipmen were newly equipped to have their most
meaningful Christmas ever.

It was during this time of anticipation and festivity that
the devastating command came to us from the main
office on campus:

ALL RELIGIOUS ACTIVITIES ARE HEREBY RESTRICTED
IMMEDIATELY BY ORDER OF THE SUPERINTENDENT.
MIDSHIPMEN ARE TO REFRAIN FROM DISCUSSING
RELIGIOUS MATTERS OUTSIDE OF THEIR OWN ROOMS
OR ATTENDING RELIGIOUS SERVICES HELD ON

*CAMPUS. ALL SERVICES ARE TO BE CONDUCTED
ONLY UNDER THE DIRECTION OF THE CHAPLAIN IN
THE ACADEMY CHAPEL.*

Yellow flyers bearing the order were tacked to every
bulletin board in Bancroft Hall and at points throughout
the campus. No explanation was given; there was just
the command. It hit us like a wave of cold water. We
were completely dumbfounded.

I called a meeting of the OCF officers in my room
immediately. Word had traveled fast. Even the non-
Christians were buzzing. At the meeting, none of the
four of us could make sense of the new restriction or
pinpoint any grievance that might have led the
superintendent to impose the regulations.

"I'll bet some atheist middie turned up the heat," said
one. "Someone must have complained about the large
number of people we were attracting to the meetings."

"We can get some Christian officers on our side,"
piped our secretary. "Plenty of high-ranking Christian
officers attend the OCF conferences. They'd put the
superintendent in his place."

Mark Henry, OCF's vice president and one of my
dearest friends, bit his lip as he listened silently. I was
just about to suggest that we enlist the help of Christian
officers to demand an explanation of the regulation
when Mark spoke up.

"We have to abide by the regulation," he said sternly.
"We'll just have to comply and disband. I'm not going to
rock the boat and jeopardize my career."

We listened to Mark's solemn words in hushed silence.
I was crushed to see he was willing to give up without a
fight.

"Well, we don't have to disband," I said. "We're
certainly entitled to some explanation. Being
midshipmen doesn't strip us of our entitlements as
American citizens. We've come too far, and our meetings

and witnessing efforts have become too important to us to just call them off like that."

"Yeah," our secretary said.

"I agree," the treasurer chipped in.

"Then count me out," Mark said, his face flushed with emotion. "I'm resigning my position in OCF and my involvement in religious activities. I've worked too hard here. Ross, you're a first classman. You of all people should see the good sense in not throwing away all you've accomplished."

Mark's words sent me reaching for my Bible.

"Mark, don't you agree with the Scripture that we should please God first and not man?" I exclaimed, holding the Bible up in one hand. "I mean, to me, serving God takes precedence over unfair regulations imposed by man, especially when the regulations stand in defiance of God's will. I've never been a rebel. I'm the biggest conformist there is, but I'm willing to put my career on the line for this. I just don't believe God will permit me to be hurt if I do."

Mark had been thumbing rapidly through the Bible as I spoke. I doubted he had even heard what I had said.

"Romans 13 instructs us to be in subjection to 'the higher powers,'" he pointed out. "No one is in authority but by the act of God, it says. Resisting authority is against God's will, Ross. There's no way I'm going to fight this regulation."

"Would it be going against God's will if the Russian people rose up en masse and defied the Russian government's laws against open Christianity?" I asserted. "I believe it's God's will to resist authority when it's corrupt, Mark. We should obey authority—but only as long as it's a lawful authority. That's how I interpret that Scripture.

"You're entitled to your feelings, Mark, but I think we should at least try to find out what's going on."

It suddenly dawned on me that the traditional prayer

vigil that we held at 4:30 on the morning of our departure for Christmas leave was only several weeks away. The time of prayer had come to be a meaningful annual event as we gathered to ask God's protection for each midshipman as he made his way home.

"What about the Christmas prayer vigil?" I questioned. "Are we just going to forget about it this year? Not me!" I said, growing angrier by the minute. "I say we hold the meeting, whether we get an explanation of this restriction or not!"

"Fine!" Mark screamed as he stood up. "But you won't get any sympathy from me when you're all tossed out of this place!"

He whirled on his heels and exited the room, slamming the door behind him.

My two colleagues sat glumly before me. I had never seen two more hangdog expressions.

"Well, what do you guys say?" I asked, bending down to peer into their faces. "Do we carry on, or not?"

The treasurer cleared his throat.

"I think you're right, Ross," he said softly. "But I think Mark is right, too. I don't think we're in any position to act too tough with the authorities. I'd like it better if we tried to negotiate with them first."

"Yeah, I think I would rather handle it diplomatically," said the other.

"And if diplomacy fails, then what?" I asked.

The treasurer shook his head. "I don't know. OCF and the Bible studies have given me more direction and inner strength than I've ever known." His chin quivered slightly as he smiled. "I guess if we're going to fight this thing, we ought to go down together."

Our secretary nodded in agreement.

"I'll do what I can to get to the bottom of this," I assured the two. "But the 4:30 Christmas prayer vigil is still on, regardless of what happens. Spread the word. Anyone who wants to come, can come."

After the two had left, I flopped down on my bunk and blew out a sigh of frustration. Outwardly, I had tried to present a solid front in my opposition to the regulation. Aside from my personal revulsion to the order, I felt like the others expected a firm stance from the leader of the OCF and NACA. But inside I felt awful.

I couldn't understand how two Christians—Mark and myself—could so intensely disagree over a matter involving the faith. I thought difficulty was supposed to bind Christians together; instead, the opposite had happened—and all to the peril of what was surely one of the Lord's most effective instruments. *One of us must be horribly wrong,* I concluded. *I guess in time the Lord will lead us to see who it is.*

Several days later, during a break in classes, I got up courage to go and see the head chaplain on campus. That morning I had been plagued by the gnawing feeling that I was opening up a colossal can of worms. Right before my own eyes I had seen myself transformed into the academy renegade. Me, Mr. Goody-Goody, Hard Work, Spit and Polish. All my life I had been a conformist, never wanting to rock the boat.

But my resolve was set. I felt I had a duty to fight for our religious freedom—a duty to God that superseded even my duty as a member of the U.S. Navy. I was certain, however, that after talking to the chaplain I would receive an explanation and be reassured that my loyalty need not be split between God and country.

I entered the chaplain's office at the rear of the chapel. I learned from his secretary that he was expected in shortly, but that his first appointment was scheduled in an hour. I wished I'd thought to call first for an appointment. I thanked the receptionist and left. As I was crossing the chapel's driveway toward the sidewalk, I noticed the chaplain coming. I hurried toward him. Upon recognizing me, a frown spread across his face.

"Chaplain, I need to speak with you when you have a

free moment," I said, pulling alongside him. He glanced at me, but continued walking at a steady pace.

"I know, Campbell," he said curtly, "but I'm late for an appointment."

"Well, can we speak sometime later today?" I asked.

"No, I don't think so," he replied as we neared his office steps. "I'm really too busy."

"I need to discuss something important with you," I reiterated earnestly.

"I know. I know," he said gruffly as he climbed the steps to his office. "You'll have to call me later."

I couldn't get over the peculiar manner in which the chaplain had acted toward me. I had never known him to be in such a huff. And then I remembered what his secretary had told me. His first appointment, for which he declared being late, hadn't been scheduled for another hour. I was certain he had guessed that I wanted to discuss the order restricting religious activities. What else would the OCF president have on his mind? "I know. I know," had been his comment.

Why would he, of all people, seem so unsympathetic? I wondered. He was stonewalling me for some reason and I knew it. The only thing I could figure was that he was under orders not to discuss the matter with members of the OCF.

The prayer vigil was less than a week away, and I had promised to get to the bottom of the new restriction. But my attempts to corner even one of the academy chaplains failed repeatedly. No one seemed to have the time to talk to me.

The usual rush to turn in assignments and study for exams before Christmas leave further hindered me from gaining an explanation for the restriction on religion. By this time I had grown so frustrated and angry I wasn't sure I wanted to hear any feeble explanations. Without question, the regulation was unfair, and, as far as I was concerned, a violation of the constitutional rights of every midshipman at Annapolis.

I couldn't wait to hold the vigil, when all of us in OCF could offer our appeal together to the Lord.

Our ten-day Christmas leave was set to begin on December 22. I was as anxious as anyone to begin my journey home for the holidays. But as I lay in bed on the night of the twenty-first, content to have completed all my assignments and semester exams, all I could think about was the early morning prayer vigil. I sat up and set my clock.

D-Day tomorrow, I said to myself. *Decision-Day. . . Defiance-Day. . . or Discharge-Day?*

That last word had an unpleasant ring to it. I certainly didn't want my rebellion to cost me more than I was willing to pay. I reached for my Bible. Recalling a passage in James that applied to my circumstances, I quickly flipped the pages and found in the third chapter what I was seeking:

But the wisdom that is from above is first pure, then peaceable, gentle, and easy to be entreated, full of mercy and good fruits, without partiality, and without hypocrisy. And the fruit of righteousness is sown in peace of them that make peace.

I put down my Bible. What the verses said to me was that even God's ultimate wisdom has an open nature. He hears our requests—our side of the story, so to speak.

My way might be right, or maybe Mark's approach was correct, I thought, *but neither of us should be so set in our stand that we refuse to hear the other. Peaceable, gentle, full of mercy—these are the traits we are to display even if we're certain a brother is dead wrong and we're right.*

The side of me calling for diplomacy won out. I leapt from my rack and hurriedly put on my bathrobe.

Fortunately, I found Mark in his room reading. The door was open so I knocked gently on the doorjamb.

"Uh, Mark, have you got a minute to talk?" I asked him. He looked over at his roommate, who was asleep. "Yeah, come on in," he whispered. "Let's keep it down, though."

"I've come to offer you a compromise," I said, smiling my most diplomatic smile. "Would you give your blessing to the vigil tomorrow morning, if we stop other religious activities indefinitely?"

"How long is indefinitely?" he said flatly.

"Until we know the superintendent's thinking behind the regulation and decide whether or not we ought to fight it," I replied.

"You intend to hold the vigil tomorrow morning anyway, don't you? Why do you want my blessing?"

"Because I don't want this to create friction between any of us, Mark," I said earnestly. "I want to compromise and handle this maturely."

Mark bit his upper lip and looked away.

"No one hates this new order any more than I do," he said. "It's wrong, and it threatens something that's really important to me, but I can't go along with holding a meeting until you've got the permission of the superintendent." He paused briefly. "I'm pleased, though, that you're going to stop OCF's activities until you get permission to go ahead."

I hadn't anticipated Mark continuing his hard line. I felt a little betrayed by my good intentions.

"Well, I'm glad you're pleased," I said sarcastically. "I had hoped you'd be willing to give a little and meet with us tomorrow."

"I'll pray here for each of you," he said.

"OK." I stood up to leave. "If you change your mind, the prayer vigil's at 0430 . . . Merry Christmas."

"Merry Christmas, Ross. Have a safe trip home."

I awoke the following morning at four o'clock, and

made my way down the hall to wash up. The sight of
lights coming on in the rooms of fellow OCF members
was heartening. Back in my room, I sat at my desk with
the reading light on and skimmed several Bible passages,
thinking about what I would say to the troops . . .
providing anyone showed up.

At 4:25 the first midshipmen sleepily began wandering
in. I felt compelled to greet each individual and thank
him for coming. Most were wearing bathrobes. Others
were already dressed in their uniforms, intending to get
an early start homeward following the meeting. All told,
well over one hundred midshipmen showed up. My
commitment to fight the order was growing stronger by
the minute.

I opened the meeting with a prayer. Although I steered
clear of making any direct reference to the order, after
praying for safe journeys home and a meaningful
Christmas, I read from Psalm 19.

" 'The law of the LORD is perfect, converting the soul:
the testimony of the LORD is sure, making wise the
simple,' " I read.

" 'The judgments of the LORD are true and righteous
altogether. More to be desired are they than gold, yea,
than much fine gold: sweeter also than honey . . .' "

Pausing briefly to look around the room, I sensed
them awaiting some dramatic statement in reference to
the new regulation. Continuing in Psalm 19, I spoke
louder for effect.

" 'Moreover by them is thy servant warned: and in
keeping of them there is great reward. Who can
understand his errors? Cleanse thou me from secret faults
. . . let them not have dominion over me: then shall I be
upright. . . .

" 'Let the words of my mouth, and the meditation of
my heart, be acceptable in thy sight. . . .' "

For several moments, no one spoke. And then the
inevitable subject—which undoubtedly was on

everyone's mind—rose to the surface. A plebe, probably the quietest and most introspective among us, boldly spoke out first.

"What really matters, then, are God's ordinances, right?" he said in a tone of muted defiance. "How we measure up to his laws is what counts—whether or not we worship him and serve him as we should."

"That's right," said another. "God comes first. Before country, before family, and before navy regulations—especially those that restrict our religious freedom."

"The thing is," another spoke up, "none of these should ever conflict with the other. I don't believe God intends them to disagree."

"So where does that leave us?" I interjected. "What do we do at this point?" The room remained quiet. No one was bold enough to suggest the direction the group should take.

"I told Mark last night I was willing to stop our activities, but only until we understood the grounds on which the regulation was made," I stated. "If we decide the order is unfair—without a legitimate basis—then I recommend we fight it."

My suggestion was greeted with approving voices and a smattering of applause.

"I say we pray about it during leave," a plebe injected sleepily.

"And go back to sleep," someone joked, nudging the plebe.

"Praying about it is certainly a good suggestion," I pointed out. "Let's pray now."

"I don't know about the rest of you," I said, laughing, as the group got to its feet after prayer, "but I need a break! Everyone have a Merry Christmas."

The farther the bus took me from the academy and the blustery cold of the East Coast, the higher my spirits soared. Anticipating the holidays and the welcome change in weather caused me to forget the storm brewing over Annapolis. Still, at times en route to Albuquerque, I was nagged by the uncertainty of how the authorities would respond to our defiant little act.

The Christmas leave accomplished a great deal toward allaying my worries. During the five days at home with my parents, my two brothers, and my sister, I hardly gave the controversy much thought. Not until my bus pulled up at the station in Annapolis did I notice a telltale moistness on my palms.

No sooner had I put my bags down in my dormitory room than someone grabbed me by the shoulder and whirled me around. It was Mark Henry.

"Are you aware that word has gotten back to the authorities that you conducted the prayer vigil?" he asked heatedly. "I really can't believe you went through with it!" His face was drained of all color. For a moment I thought he was going to hit me.

"You know you've risked having OCF discontinued for good at Annapolis! Why didn't you just get permission? The superintendent probably would have given it to you."

"Hold it, Mark!" I yelled back. "Just hold it, will you? We did what we thought was right. We'll just have to see what the consequences will be."

"Well, you won't have to wait long," he shot back. "They're looking for you now."

"Who?" I demanded. My stomach did a little flip. It was the feeling I used to get when I'd broken something at home or been caught playing hooky.

"Some young chaplain was in here looking for you," he replied. "I'm sure the head chaplain wants you on the carpet."

"Fine, Mark," I said angrily. "Thanks for the information."

A hurt expression came to his face. He turned and walked out the door. "Several men in OCF have already received warnings from the superintendent and the chief chaplain," Mark said, turning around. "It's not my intention to hurt anybody. I simply want to save everyone from a lot of heartache. We've already been given fair warning."

For the next several days, I expected an order to report to the superintendent or one of the chaplains, but one never came. For a while, I basked in my perceived good fortune, thinking that while we hadn't exactly beaten the order, we'd at least defied it and come out unscathed. As the weeks passed, however, and the OCF leaders held true to the decision to halt activities until more was known, my relief turned to bitterness. All of us began to experience a terrible feeling of oppression.

What made things worse for me was that I had fallen under a barrage of assignments required for graduation, again frustrating any efforts to arrange appointments with the authorities. After being denied appointments by the secretaries of the superintendent and the head chaplain, I finally realized I couldn't arrange a mutually acceptable time to hold these meetings even if there were forty-eight hours in the day.

Not the least of my pressing assignments was my senior term paper—a major requirement to graduate—for which I still had no topic. With my mind clouded with worries about the futures of OCF and NACA at Annapolis, I found myself drawing a blank each time I tried to identify a subject that would interest me. Finally, I made an appointment with my English professor, hoping he could suggest a subject on which to write.

Dr. Bob Thurgood, a former navy officer, had become something of a fixture at Annapolis. None of us knew much about his military past; he seemed reluctant to discuss his service during World War II.

But one thing was certain about him: He loved conflict, at least the kind he was capable of stirring up in the classroom. Nothing gave him more pleasure than igniting a heated debate between two or more students over some current issue.

"Come in and sit down, Campbell," Dr. Thurgood said upon seeing me at the door of his office.

"So you're having a little trouble coming up with a topic, huh?" He looked at me patronizingly over his reading glasses. "Well, I love brainstorming. Let's see if we can't get a storm rolling in that head of yours."

"I've really drawn a blank," I said. "I guess I'm a little drained."

He sat back in his leather chair and put his hands behind his head. "OK, tell me your interests. Let's see, which is it—science, navigation, engineering, things like that, or. . . . What exactly do you like to do in your free time? What do you like to read?"

"I don't get a lot of time to read for pleasure, but when I do, I enjoy studying the Bible."

"The Bible?" He thought for a moment. "The Bible contains some great literature. Is there any aspect of your religion that might interest you to write about?"

"I don't know if it would be a topic for a paper, but the midshipmen have been restricted from holding religious activities. Chapel services and meetings under the direct supervision of the chaplain are all that's permitted."

"That's your theme right there," he said matter-of-factly. "I think you'd do a good job with it."

"You think so?" I asked innocently. "What would the topic be—regulation of religion at the U.S. Naval Academy?"

"Precisely. There's an issue of constitutional rights, it seems to me."

The more I thought about it, the more sold I became on the idea. "Great. That's what I'll do," I said enthusiastically. "I don't know why I didn't think of it before. I guess I thought it was . . . inappropriate to put the ordeal on paper.

"Thanks, professor," I said, bounding out of my chair. "I'm going to get to the research right away."

Hurrying down the hall, I realized I would be able to kill two birds with one stone: I could write my paper and, in the process, uncover the primary cause of the regulation that had put such a damper on Christian life in the dormitory.

At the bottom of the steps in the English building, I suddenly asked myself where I was headed in such a hurry. I didn't have the vaguest idea of where to begin my search for information. I would need facts about both past and present religious activities at Annapolis. "Jim Wilson," I muttered to myself. "If anyone can put me on the right track, he can."

And, I thought, *I'm going to need a book on the constitution.*

Minutes later I entered the off-campus Christian bookstore owned by the academy OCF rep. Because of my hectic classroom schedule, Jim and I hadn't crossed paths recently. I was anxious to discuss the new restrictive order with him. His face lit up when he saw me.

"Ross," he beamed. "I was just thinking about you. What can I do for you? Let's go back to my office and talk."

I got right to the point of my visit.

"I need you to help me obtain any files relating to religious activities, past and present, on campus," I said. "I'm writing my senior term paper on the restriction of religion at the academy."

"Brother!" he sighed, slumping back into his chair. "Do you expect any flak from this?"

"Not really," I said casually. "I don't intend anyone to read it except Professor Thurgood. He suggested I use the topic."

"Yeah, and I wonder why," Jim said. "He loves to get a good fight started. I hope you're not doing something that will get you in trouble."

"Well, we at Bancroft wanted to uncover the reasoning behind the regulation anyway," I said. "It's not a fair order, and the guys want to fight it. But first we have to find out what in the world's going on."

"I can tell you it was an order that was written with very little support among the faculty on campus," Jim said. "It stands on shaky ground."

"Great. Jim, we can beat it. Right now I need any files you have on Annapolis religious activities. And I need references on constitutional rights regarding religious freedom. I want to get started right away."

Jim rummaged through several filing cabinets and produced three full folders containing minutes of OCF meetings, articles from the academy newspaper, memos, and sundry other items dating back to his navy days.

"Thanks, buddy," I said with a grin. "I'll return these shortly. I need to get started on my outline."

"Let me know how things go," he responded. "Call me if I can help. And Ross . . ." His eyes softened and a fatherly look came to his face. "Be careful."

Jim's folders had a wealth of valuable material, information that would not only help me with the paper, but also make a case for the reinstatement of religious activities. Documents, memos, letters from high-ranking officers, articles—all pertaining to OCF and its excellent work—gave me the ammunition I needed.

Surprisingly, in the weeks ahead, I had little trouble obtaining files in the chaplain's office regarding OCF and other academy religious activities. I soon learned that Jim Wilson was running interference for me at the chaplain's office. Jim was one of God's most dedicated servants; it was through his witness that my misconceptions of Christianity had been stripped away and I had met Jesus as a real person. Now when I desperately needed some guidance, he was there for me again.

As a part of my research, I made appointments with members of the faculty who I knew were Christians. Several of them informed me of a situation I had expected all along.

"I can tell you this much, Ross," my math professor

said in a hushed voice near the end of our session. "All this originated with the head chaplain. He saw some problems with the fervor you guys were creating. He approached me about the regulation before it was written, and I told him I was totally against it. But he persevered."

"I suspected that," I said. "I can't believe the academy chaplain would try to undermine religious activities on campus and restrict our constitutional rights. He probably felt threatened."

"I think that was part of it, Ross."

"Well, thanks," I said. "Now I know what we're up against."

For two weeks I feverishly worked to organize and present the enormous amount of material I had accumulated. Finally, I was through. The paper would be good enough to get a passing grade, but whether it achieved an A hardly mattered. The catharsis it had afforded me was worth the effort alone. And I had accomplished a great deal in my mission to uncover the culprits responsible for the order.

They don't know how shaky the ground is beneath them, I thought before falling asleep on the eve of the paper's deadline.

When I dropped the paper on Dr. Thurgood's desk the next day, he looked up and smiled mischievously.

"Is this good enough to really shake 'em up?" he laughed.

"Shake who up?"

"The super and the chaplain over at headquarters."

"I didn't intend for them to read it," I pointed out. "But I think some of the facts in there could help the case for religious freedom, if that's what you mean."

"Well, good luck. I know you've worked hard on it. You'll get your grades next week."

I left the class wondering about the professor's cryptic statements.

I picked up my grades the following week, but my regulations paper was not in the stack with the others. I found only a note with my name on it: "Good work. Your paper deserved to be read by some people who I thought could help you, Campbell. I hope you don't mind. Dr. Thurgood."

I felt the sweat building on my brow.

Still, I thought, *it's material they all know anyway. I just hope they understand I had a need to know.*

I figured they couldn't come down on me too hard for merely assimilating the facts about religious activities on campus and defending freedom of religion. I didn't convince myself, though.

Three days later, a plebe messenger came to my door.

"Ross Campbell?" he said.

"Yes," I replied.

"This is for you."

The message requested my presence at a hearing in the office of Capt. William F. Bringle, the academy commandant, at 1300 hours (1:00 P.M.) tomorrow. My palms began to sweat. I considered going directly to Jim Wilson or some of my Christian buddies and informing them of the development, but decided simply to play it cool and keep the others out of it. It was my paper; it was my battle.

The next day, fifteen minutes early, I stepped up to the desk of the commandant's secretary and informed her that I was there for my appointment.

"Go right in," she said.

"Now?" I gulped.

"Yes. The commandant is expecting you."

I swung open the large oak door and walked into the carpeted office. The commandant looked up. He was holding the paper in his hands.

"Campbell?"

"Yes, sir, Midshipman Ross Campbell."

"You're early; that's good," he said warmly. "Sit down."

Captain Bringle's pleasant manner put me at ease immediately. I had the feeling that the commandant was on my side, and, perhaps, even a Christian.

"Campbell, this is very good," he said, holding my term paper up in one hand. "Professor Thurgood gave you an A on it, and you deserve it."

He flipped through the paper to the last page. " 'Very well written. Very good.' The professor has some nice things to say about you here on the last page.

"You probably understand the constitution now more than most people," he said, looking up suddenly to reveal a smile.

"The professor feels like you people are getting a raw deal . . . and so do I."

I could have jumped up and kissed him. The regulation, it seemed, was as good as torn up.

"Thank you, sir," I said. "We've never tried to force our beliefs on anyone on campus or off. The activities just continued to grow. They've meant a lot to a lot of people. We'd appreciate anything you can do."

The commandant's manner suddenly became stern.

"There are a lot of changes I would like to see made here and throughout the navy," he said. "But there are proper channels to pursue in attempting to make those changes. I hope you won't feel the need to write a paper or stir things up every time you run across a navy regulation that doesn't suit you.

"Regulations are for our own good. That's not to say they're all perfect. But there's a proper way to bring about change."

"Yes, sir," I said, a little shaken by his reprimanding tone. "This is the only regulation I have trouble with." I regretted my choice of words. I hoped he didn't see me as a rebel.

"Well, I'll see that proper channels are pursued in this matter," he stated. "While the regulation is still valid, I expect you and all the midshipmen to abide by it. Understood?"

"Yes, sir."

He stood up with a big smile on his face and extended his hand. "You're a good man, Campbell. Keep up the good work."

I shook his hand and saluted. I felt more relieved than I'd felt in the last two months. I had the sensation that the Lord was working through my efforts; unquestionably, the paper had been written with his help and guidance. Now, all we had to do was wait.

Ten days or so passed, and no word whatever came down about the regulation. On the surface things seemed pretty calm, but all of us middies were convinced that a real furor was going on behind closed doors. The particularly cool treatment I received from the chaplain's office indicated a tempest was swirling at the top.

I was a bit unnerved to get a particularly harsh glare from the chief chaplain one afternoon as I passed him at a distance on campus, but I read his expression as a favorable sign. I was dying to find out what all of this rather strained behavior meant. Less than four weeks before my graduation, on an especially balmy early spring afternoon, I received the almost unbelievable news.

I was seated on a bench outside the PX reading, when I heard Mark Henry hailing me from quite a distance away. This struck me as unusual: He'd been avoiding me, so I'd heard from others, after learning I had actually written my term paper on the regulation of religion on campus. But now he called to me like a long lost relative.

"Ross!" he shouted as discreetly as possible. I stood up. He was out of breath when he got to me. "Where have you been?" he asked, pulling me by the arm out to the open sidewalk.

"Right here," I said, astonished by his uncharacteristically excited demeanor. "What's wrong?"

"Nothing's wrong. Haven't you heard?" he said

chuckling. "You've won! I can't believe you had the gall to do it, but you've won!"

"What have I won?" I said. Suddenly it occurred to me that he was referring to the paper I'd written. "Are they reversing the order?"

"Not yet," he said. "But it looks good. The chief of naval operations, Admiral Arleigh Burke, will be here in a week to conduct a full investigation of the matter. I can't believe what you've done. You've won, Ross!"

Mark went on to say that the paper had gone to the secretary of the navy in Washington. Apparently, things had started to move pretty fast in our favor following that. I was speechless.

"Who told you this?" I blurted out finally.

"You won't believe who. Professor Thurgood. Can you believe it? He told me to tell you when I picked up an English assignment. He seemed tickled to death that he had gotten everything so stirred up."

"Wow, Mark. I can't believe it either. That's super!"

I wanted to dance a jig. The attention my paper had received was obviously a boost to my ego. But mostly I was glad the ordeal was nearly over and religious freedom would be restored. God had found a way— despite all the divisiveness among the brass on campus and even among us midshipmen—to bring about justice and align things with his purposes.

"You know, Mark, God would have found a way to straighten all of this out, regardless of which way we'd turned," I said. "I always felt it was impossible for two Christians to disagree without one being right and the other being wrong. But we were both right."

"I think I know what you're saying, Ross. He would have honored us either way. He'd have gotten through to the superintendent and the chaplain's office somehow even if we'd taken my approach and toed the line."

Mark and I walked back to the dorm together, and spent the rest of the afternoon and evening discussing our years at Annapolis, our commitment to Christ, and our futures as naval officers.

Just before taps, as Mark was leaving my room, he turned and smiled.

"Whaddya think we ought to use as the Scripture for our last OCF Bible study in this place?"

"I'll leave it up to you," I replied with a chuckle. "Remember, you haven't been to a meeting in months. It's your turn to teach."

➡ *Consider it all joy . . . when you encounter various trials* (James 1:2, NASB).

➡ *Out of difficulties grow miracles* (Jean dè la Bruyers).

CHAPTER

AN UNWELCOME ASSIGNMENT

"Hey, Campbell, how'd you like a blind date?" my roommate Dave Bishop asked.

"Who? Where? What's she look like?" I queried. We were in Pensacola for summer aviation training—"to get a taste of what it's like to be a pilot," as our commanding officer had put it. There wasn't much to do after hours, so Dave's proposal sounded interesting.

"She's a friend of my girl, Freddie. Cute blue-eyed brunette, Freddie says. She's a Christian, too. We'll go to their church Sunday night, then over to Freddie's house afterwards."

I won't say I fell in love with Pat on our first date. But we were together enough that summer to make me believe I wanted to keep the relationship going.

Two years later, and three days after I graduated from the naval academy and was commissioned an ensign, Pat and I said our "I do's" in the First Baptist Church of Pensacola. After the honeymoon, we took up residence in an apartment in Long Beach, California, where I was promoted to lieutenant junior grade and assigned as a gunnery division officer to the carrier, the USS *Princeton.*

When my ship sailed for a six-month western Pacific cruise, Pat went back to stay with her folks in Pensacola, which is where Carey, our first child, was born. I didn't see my new daughter until she was three months old.

Nothing is ever settled when you're in the navy. We tried to pretend it was and rented a little house in Long Beach. Pat enrolled in college, even though we realized my new orders could come at any time.

When the assignment came at the end of my tour with the USS *Princeton,* I could hardly wait to tell Pat. I decided to stretch out the suspense after I arrived home with the orders.

Pat squirmed in her chair like a child being teased with a long-awaited surprise. It really wasn't fair to keep her hanging, but I was feeling especially playful in light of the good news I held in the manilla envelope stamped "Confidential."

I peered mischievously at her over the folder containing my orders. Fourteen-month-old Carey was happily unconcerned about our discussion. She sat at Pat's feet, contentedly playing with her toys.

"Well, where would you like to be stationed next?" I asked nonchalantly.

"I'd like to stay in southern California and finish up my degree," she said, adding with a shrug and a sly smile, "but 'whither thou goest, I will go.' "

I couldn't hold back the truth any longer.

"How does it feel to be the wife of the new executive officer of the USS *Rogers,* landing ship tank (LST), home ported in San Diego?" I asked matter-of-factly.

"Oh, Ross, that's fantastic!" Pat squealed as she leapt to her feet. She ran over to where I was sitting, plopped down in my lap, and threw her arms around me.

She leaned back to view my expression. "You're not joking, are you?" she asked suspiciously.

"Nope. See for yourself." I handed her my orders. She scanned the top paper briefly until she was satisfied.

"An executive officer," she exclaimed proudly. "Ross, it's exactly what you wanted. I was afraid you'd get orders to a WestPac ship or something."

"Best of all," I added, "this LST performs training maneuvers only off the West Coast."

I sat back in my chair and put my arms behind my head.

"No more long cruises for me," I said. "And an executive officer. It really looks like I'm going someplace in this man's navy."

Pat laughed. "I guess our ship's finally come in."

My good mood carried over into the next week and the week after that. The usual drudgery of my mostly administrative work as a gunnery division officer aboard the USS *Princeton* seemed a snap.

The two of us had been on needles and pins awaiting the news of my transfer; now, with this choice set of orders, we could relax for the first time in weeks. I was especially happy for Pat, because she'd be allowed to remain in the California school system and complete her studies at San Diego State.

I was certain I couldn't be any happier than I would be aboard the USS *Rogers*. For now, there appeared to be nothing to tarnish this demonstration of the navy's faith in me. They trusted me to meet a sizable challenge.

Less than a month from the date I was due to report to my new ship in San Diego, a message came for me to report to the chief petty officer in personnel. I'd spent much of the beautiful June day soaking in the sunshine while I oversaw a general cleanup of the guns and prepared for our gunnery practice the next day.

I scrambled happily down the hatchway ladders to the personnel office. My ebullient mood had been building these past few days. I had a good life, a wonderful wife, and a great career that I'd carved out through hard work and endurance.

In my present state, I was oblivious to any thought that the rug was about to be pulled out from under me. I quickly suspected something was up, however, when the chief of personnel invited me to sit down in his tiny office.

"Lieutenant Campbell, new orders have just come in for you," the non-com said solemnly. "Your old ones to the USS *Rogers* in San Diego have been changed."

My first inclination was to think that my orders had been improved, since the navy had shown such high regard for me in the first place. I was on a roll. "OK, what are they?"

"Uh. . . ." He hesitated slightly. "You're being assigned as gunnery officer of the USS *Daniel A. Joy* out of Chicago. It's a naval destroyer escort. Uh, it's a naval reserve training ship."

"What?!" I reacted with a yell.

He recoiled only slightly at my outburst, as though he was used to being a frequent bearer of bad news.

"Yes, sir," he continued tersely, "but you've been ordered to report first to San Diego for six weeks of gunnery school."

"Mister, you've got to be mistaken! I'm due to become the exec of the USS *Rogers* next week!" I snatched the papers from his hand. "Let me see this."

But as I read over the orders, it was obvious that there had been no mistake. The special orders out of the U.S. Navy Bureau of Personnel in Washington, D.C., were dated yesterday. It was official.

I flipped the order back to the chief and sunk into my chair, crushed by the sudden turn of events.

The chief respectfully paused several moments. "We'll, uh, keep you posted, Lieutenant. You report to gunnery school in one month."

I was absolutely speechless. I stared at the chief and drew in a deep breath, letting it out slowly. After a minute, I stood up.

"Well, I want you to validate this, chief," I said in a defeated voice. "You have to admit it's a little unusual to change orders like this at the last minute."

"Sir, everything's in order," he responded. "You know how the navy is. It's been done before."

"Yeah, but not to me." I threw aside the blue drape hanging in the hatchway and walked briskly out of personnel, unconcerned that my little tirade caused every head to look up as I passed.

It was nearly 1600 (4:00 P.M.) and quitting time, so I exited the ship and headed toward my car parked nearby. *How's Pat going to take this?* I wondered. *Chicago . . . with a fourteen-month-old baby. . . She's going to hate Chicago. And I'm back where I started, as a gunnery officer—aboard a reservist training ship, no less. I know I'm going to hate it.*

I drove home, still bewildered by the news I'd just received, periodically feeling pangs of anxiety and anger as the image of dirty Chicago surfaced in my thoughts. Just then, I recalled something Pat had said during a drive through south Chicago following our honeymoon. We were en route to California and the USS *Princeton*, passing slums and belching smokestacks, and rows of unsightly wires and electrical metal towers, when Pat had announced, "This is definitely one place I'd never want to live."

I'm dragging her face to face with her greatest nightmare, I thought.

On my way inside the house, I scooped up the paper

on the front porch and shook it open. "Berlin Crisis Deepens, as Vienna Summit Fails," read the banner headline on page one. The meeting between Soviet Premier Kruschev and President Kennedy to discuss the flight of East Germans into West Germany had ended in discord.

Pat kissed me on the cheek just as I stepped in the front door.

"Hi," I said, glancing upward momentarily from another story, which bore the headline: "Kennedy Puts 145,000 National Guardsmen, Reservists on Alert."

"Everybody's got problems," I said, flipping the paper to an empty chair.

"We don't," Pat cooed. "You've got me and I've got you. And we've got Carey." She stopped suddenly in her tracks, noticing the troubled look on my face.

"Ross, what's wrong?"

I slumped to the couch. "They've changed my orders, that's what's wrong." There was no gentle way to break the news.

"Pat, we're going to Chicago," I blurted out. "I've been assigned as gunnery officer of the *Daniel A. Joy,* a naval reserve destroyer out of Chicago."

Pat's mouth dropped wide open. She sat down hard on the arm of the couch. "I can't believe it! If you're joking . . ."

I looked up at her and shook my head. "First, I've got six weeks in San Diego in gunnery school."

Throughout dinner, Pat looked as crestfallen as I knew she would be. But despite the prospect of having to set up residence in metropolitan Chicago during the stifling summer heat, as always, she tried to put on her best face.

Realizing that an aunt and her family lived a few hours from Chicago in Elyria, Ohio, seemed to give a boost to her spirits. "We'll just do what we have to do, Ross," she said finally. "We can visit my aunt and uncle. They'll love to see us."

I'd seen some pretty sturdy personalities thus far in my life, especially in the navy—people who almost seem to welcome change and don't flinch a bit when it comes roaring down upon them—but not one had anything on my wife of barely two years. I was astonished at her ability to roll with such a devastating punch.

In about a month's time, Pat's resiliency—and mine—were sorely tested as we moved from our one-bedroom house in Long Beach to temporary living quarters in a Quonset hut in San Diego. It was agony knowing that each passing day of gunnery school brought us closer to our scheduled departure from southern California.

By the end of July, the time for our eastward trek was upon us. The navy had packed and shipped our furniture to Chicago from Long Beach six weeks before.

I'd watched as the van pulled away from the curb in front of our house, fighting the temptation to halt the vehicle, pull everything off it myself, and inform the navy I wasn't going anywhere.

I dreaded the long, long drive that remained after we packed our Tempest station wagon with the rest of our belongings. Our first stop would be Pensacola, Florida, where Carey would stay for a week with Pat's folks. They'd meet us later in Ohio after we found an apartment.

Next would be the slums and smokestacks, and the rows of wires and electrical towers that Pat pretended not to hate anymore.

We drove as far as we could from the sight of the industrial south end of Chicago and still be within commuting distance of the docks. Without any previous knowledge of the area, we managed to find a brand new, two-bedroom apartment in what was then one of the safest districts near downtown Chicago, roughly ten miles west of the famed Loop.

Having two bedrooms delighted Pat, and she quickly began making curtains—and friends. The following Sunday, at the invitation of a neighbor family, we attended Melrose Park Bible Church. It didn't take us long to be accepted into the warm fellowship of the congregation. If only this kind of company might have spilled over to the docks where my new duty station awaited.

Even as Lake Michigan and Navy Pier came into view, I still couldn't believe what was happening to me. Slightly more than three months ago, I was the happiest man in the U.S. Navy. Now I felt like its biggest goat.

Out of the cab window to my right towered the gray Chicago skyline. To my left was Lake Michigan, dotted by yachts and sailboats, their bells and bleached sails quivering in the city's famous wind. Navy Pier, adorned by sunbathing civilians and sidewalk vendors with their colorful carts, stretched out into the expansive lake.

And plunked down right in the middle of this unmatchable scene was an old navy destroyer, so tired and seaworn it appeared to lean on the dock for support. If I had felt slighted at any time in my career before, now I really felt like I'd been put out to pasture.

"That's why the lady is a tramp . . . ," the taxi's radio blared. The driver's head bobbed to the beat until the taxi had come to a complete stop.

"Six bucks and a quarter, Mac," the cabbie said, turning in his seat to face me.

"This is Navy Pier, isn't it?" I asked foolishly, already knowing the answer.

"None other. Dat's the *Joy* right dere," he said in his thick Chicago tongue. "Dat's your ship, ain't it?" He studied my uniform, trying to determine my rank.

"Lieutenant, junior grade," I said, slightly annoyed at his smugness.

"Yeah, yeah. I was gonna say dat," he replied offhandedly.

"Yeah, dis is your ship. The pride of Chicago," he laughed, wiping his brow with a soiled handkerchief.

"Adds new meaning to the term 'tin can,' don't it? Naw, jes kiddin'."

He got out of his door and hoisted my green duffle bag and a small gym bag from the trunk, dropping them at my feet.

I handed him eight dollars. "Keep it," I said curtly.

"Yeah, thanks, uh, Cap'n," he said, climbing back in his seat. "Hope youse like it here. Dat's a great ole ship, the *Joy*." With that, he slammed his door and roared off in a cloud of fumes.

"The *Joy*, my foot," I muttered miserably to myself. "I don't see any joy around here." I snatched up the gym bag and my duffle bag, which seemed heavier than I remembered, and walked toward the ship.

The tremendous floating hulk of steel made this incongruous scene—public lakeshore beaches on one side and grime-stained skyscrapers on the other—look downright surreal. It was almost as if these two worlds, which could operate successfully without each other, had collided by accident and remained slammed together.

Just before reaching the ship's gangplank, I accidentally kicked an empty whiskey bottle lying along the curb.

Brother, I thought, *what has the navy got me into?*

Midway up the gangplank I could see the lake's distant banks and sailboats gliding effortlessly in the breeze. The summer scenes made me long for California's oceanside, where the beaches are less obstructed by concrete and spared the ice and snow of Chicago's winter.

A sudden, stiff blast of wind slapped me back to my senses. I hurried up the gangplank to the covered quarterdeck where the officer of the day stands watch to receive the crew and visitors while the ship's in port.

To my amazement, no one was standing guard at the officer's podium. Dropping my things with a thud, I angrily turned to face the ship's aft portion and render the customary salute to the flag. But no flag was in sight. "I certainly hope they're flying the flag!" I said to myself.

Quickly, I began looking around to find the first open compartment. *Forget the business of getting situated and meeting the command,* I thought. *I'm going to get some answers first.*

The first compartment I came to contained two sailors. They were leaning back in their chairs, throwing darts at a picture tacked to a dartboard.

"Missed!" one of them said, as his dart landed well off its mark. The picture bore the face of a young woman. The next dart stuck in the vicinity of the girl's chin.

"Ah ha! Gotcha this time," one of the men howled. The two men exploded into maniacal laughter. "That'll teach ya to double-cross me."

Just then another sailor burst into the room. His hair was dripping wet, and he was dressed only in his undershorts—not the navy issue of regular white boxer skivvies, but red polka-dotted undershorts. A second sailor dressed only in his trousers was in hot pursuit, carrying a twisted towel. The two tore around the room, knocking over chairs and tables and sending ashtrays and cards flying.

Whack! went the towel, as the pursuing sailor missed his prey and caught one of the chairs instead. A second flip of the towel caught the sailor on the thigh. *Whack!*

"Ahhh!" the pursued man screamed in pain. "I give! I give!"

Unmercifully, the towel popper let another assault fly. "Yeooww!" the other man squawked, rubbing the back of his leg. "Quit it, will ya?"

The two were barreling in my direction. I put up my hands for protection from where I stood on the other side of the hatchway. They caught themselves before crashing into me, and stood frozen like two naughty children who had just been caught in the act of some devilish deed.

"Hey," said the dart-thrower, noticing me. "A new addition."

It's customary, sometimes strictly required depending upon the command, for enlisted men to come to attention when an officer enters the room. I would have been lucky to get a Bronx cheer from this bunch. The two men tilted back in their seats did, at least, let the legs of their chairs drop to the deck.

Judging from their carefree attitudes (and their underwear), I was certain these men were reservists. Weekend warriors. It's doubtful they would have shown me any more respect if I'd been the commander of the sixth fleet. As it was I was only a lieutenant, junior grade. I was sure they'd seen my type before— practically just out of school and still slightly wet behind the ears.

"You regular navy?" the towel popper asked.

"Yes, as a matter of fact, I am," I said.

"Hey, things are picking up around here. You're the second regular navy officer in two days. Well, welcome aboard Mr. . . ." He squinted his eyes and craned his neck to see my nameplate. ". . . Mr. Campbell," he read. "Welcome to the *Joy*."

"Or as we call it," the other dart thrower piped up, "the *Joy Ship*."

"I call it the *Jolly Roger*," said the man in polka-dotted shorts, "because we're all a bunch of pirates." He closed one eye and hunched his back. "Right, mateys?" he growled.

"Yeah, right," I said, trying to hide my impatience. "Who's supposed to be on guard at the quarterdeck?"

"Beats me," said one of the dart throwers. "Someone was there when I came aboard this morning. He probably went to the head."

"Well, somebody needs to be there at all times," I said. I poked my head out and saw that the guard had in fact returned. "OK, you guys carry on," I said, forcing a smile. "And if you should run out of darts, how about cleaning up this compartment a little bit?"

"OK, sir," the other dart thrower said casually.

"Where can I find Commander Robert Phelps?" I asked the two men closest to me.

"The captain?" the man with the towel replied.

"Yes."

"Uh, he's only around on weekends, actually. He'll be here tomorrow for our cruise."

"All right, thanks." I backed out of the compartment, shaking my head. "What a zoo," I moaned to myself.

"Mr. Campbell," one of the men called out.

"Yes?" I answered from a short distance.

"The exec, Lieutenant Commander Smith, is aboard, I think."

"Thanks."

I headed straight for the Officer of the Deck, who happened to be an enlisted man—a boatswain's mate, second-class. After putting in a call to the bridge, he informed me that Lieutenant Commander Smith would meet me in his cabin.

"Can you tell me how to get to his cabin?" I asked.

"Uh, not really; I've only been on the ship once before," he answered.

I'd have been shocked at the sight of the petty officer's overweight form and slightly unkempt appearance on any other U.S. Navy vessel, but as it was, this character fit in perfectly with the others. *Weekend warriors,* I thought again.

"Never mind," I said. "I'll find it. Thanks."

"Yes, sir," he said enthusiastically, snapping a rather awkward salute.

"Carry on," I said, returning his salute. I didn't know whether to laugh or cry. I decided to withhold doing either until after my meeting with the executive officer.

Ordinarily, on Friday afternoon you'd expect to see much of the crew getting ready to go on liberty. But as this was a reservist ship—a fact of which I had little difficulty reminding myself—the crew was actually arriving for work . . . or whatever it was these people did.

As I made my way up to the bridge, I couldn't believe the disrepair around me. "This ship has got to be pre-World War II," I figured.

Occasionally, I would come across a party of young reservists mopping or sweeping their weekend sleeping quarters under the command of a zealous third-class petty officer. But for the most part I saw utter chaos.

My ire grew with each step up the final ladder to the bridge. By the time I located the executive officer's cabin, I was really worked up into a lather. I tried to picture the exec and this Commander Phelps, and how in the world the two could permit these substandard conditions to persist, even if this was only a reserve training ship.

Unbelievable, I thought as I knocked several times on the cabin door.

After a moment, there was a muffled voice. "Come in."

Lieutenant Commander Smith, a slender, clean-cut man in his early thirties, was slouched behind a small desk in the rear of his quarters when I walked in. He'd apparently been reading and dozing.

"Yes?" he said sleepily.

"Mr. Smith?" I inquired, "I'm Lieutenant, j. g. Campbell." I was reluctant to say the next words. "Arriving for duty."

"Yes, yes. Lieutenant Campbell," he said cheerfully. "I've got your orders right here. Been lookin' over 'em." He pulled up a chair for me and sat back down at his desk.

"Welcome aboard," he said a little self-consciously. He raked his hand over the mussed tuft of hair on his head. I could see he was uncomfortable.

"Um . . . we're glad to have you," he said at last. He

seemed to be struggling for the right words. "I know we're not what you're used to, but, uh, we . . . we're gonna do our best to get these men ready."

I felt my cheeks begin to flush. I wanted to say my piece right then, but I held my tongue.

"The navy seems to have some big plans for us, though I'm not sure what they are yet," he continued. "You're gonna be a big help to us, I'm sure, Lieutenant."

"I'll do my best to help. I have to admit, I'm not quite used to . . . this."

Suddenly, I felt sorry for the man. He was no doubt embarrassed to have an outsider see the unimpressive condition of the ship and its crew.

"Lieutenant, I'm well aware that this is only a reservist ship, but navy reserve or not, the crew seems to be a little . . ."

"A little on the crazy side?" he laughed.

"Yes, sir. That's kind of what I had in mind."

"They're really a harmless bunch." He eyed me intently, as if he were slightly annoyed. "We don't have any serious problems. But they could be a little more serious about their duties, I guess."

The lieutenant commander rubbed his chin and stood up. He walked to a nearby table, where he retrieved and lit his pipe, and sat down on the table's corner.

"Mr. Campbell, you need to understand a few things," he said. His face grew suddenly stern. "We're not all spit and polish around here; we can't expect these men to be. They're here for three days a month, and that's not time enough to instill a lot of discipline.

"But they're a good bunch. They're not mean." He stopped suddenly and appeared to wrestle with what to say next.

"I think I know why you've been sent here," he said quietly. "You're the second regular navy officer to arrive in two days. Another lieutenant arrived yesterday to serve as our engineering officer. The navy is going to send us on some sort of extended cruise shortly, and you two men are obviously a big part of what the navy intends to do."

"What is it, some sort of shakedown operation?"

He put down his pipe and paused again.

"I just don't know," he said through a puff of smoke. "A good part of the navy's reserve ships are being readied. I don't know what it means. I suppose the alert in Berlin has something to do with it. President Kennedy has something in mind."

I started to speak, but he cut me off.

"We'll get ready, Mr. Campbell," he said. "And you'll help us a great deal. But just understand our limitations. Don't come down too hard and make your life miserable.

"Fair enough?"

I was frankly stunned by what I considered to be a poor defense—a load of excuses, really—for a motley crew of sailors . . . and a bucket of bolts. *If this ship is going to make a cruise,* I thought, *that's all the more reason to have discipline on board. Going to sea with a crew right out of* Mr. Roberts *would be more than I could bear.*

"I'll do my best to fit in," I said in a slightly exasperated tone. "I'm ready to help in any way I can." I immediately regretted the Pollyannaish ring to my remarks, but I couldn't think of anything else to say.

"Fine, Lieutenant," he said. "We're all a big family. These men really do very well during our little weekend cruises on Lake Michigan. We'll be going out tomorrow."

Lake Michigan's not the open sea, I thought. *I presume he knows that.*

"Is your family here?" he asked with a smile.

"Yes, sir, they are."

"And you've found a place to stay?"

"Yes, sir, in Melrose Park."

"Great, great. That's a nice little neighborhood. A lot of ethnic charm."

"We've been so busy getting moved in, we haven't really gotten to know anyone yet. Just the people we've met at the church we found."

He nodded thoughtfully. "I saw in your orders that you've served as a chaplain's assistant. You wouldn't be interested in serving as our chaplain, would you?"

"Well, sure, if you need one," I answered.

The lieutenant commander stood up and smiled.

"We're glad to have you aboard," he said. "We feel complete, now that we've got us a chaplain."

"Yes, sir," I said with a grin.

As I was leaving he remarked, "Don't forget now. We work Saturdays around here. We're shoving off at 1000 tomorrow for a training cruise. You can find a cabin for yourself on down to stow your gear."

"Right. Thank you, sir."

I closed the door behind me and stood motionless for a moment in the empty passageway. I sighed deeply. My arms hung limply at my side as I let my shoulders sag. I needed to go home and digest all of this.

I felt my pants pockets to see if I had a dime for a call home. I couldn't wait to speak to Pat, but I dreaded having to fill her in on what I'd just found.

The ongoing ruckus on the decks below was audible through the ladder hatch to my left. I'd attended fraternity parties that sounded more reserved. "These men think this is some sort of floating camp resort, or something," I mumbled aloud. *They think this is all one big joke—a joy ride,* I thought, cringing at the pun.

I wanted to kick myself for not being more assertive about the poor condition of the men and the decks below. *So what if he'd gotten offended or angry?* I concluded. *There's nothing disrespectful about expressing one's opinion.*

Then I wondered what role my faith would play in my ability to handle all of this. *How on earth can I ever be happy here? What purpose can I possibly serve aboard this rust bucket? What has God led me into?*

Making my way down the passageway, I suddenly realized the lieutenant commander hadn't instructed me where I could find my office. I began opening door after door on the officers' deck, dragging my gear after me. Each cabin was dirtier and in more disarray than the next. I thought foolishly that my cabin would be the one I'd find swept and mopped, with clean sheets and blankets stowed on the bunk. The last door I tried in the section was locked.

This must be mine, I thought. *They've put it under lock and key for safekeeping. But who's got the key?*

"Who's there?" a voice shouted from behind the metal door.

"Never mind," I called out. "Wrong cabin."

In a moment, the door swung open and I stood face to face with a fellow Annapolis graduate, Roger Anderson. The silver bar on his collar told me he was a lieutenant. We recognized one another immediately.

"Roger Anderson," I said with a grin. "I hope I didn't disturb you."

"No, no, not at all," he said. "Ross Campbell, isn't it? Have you just been assigned here?"

"Well, no," I kidded, "actually I'm selling vacuum cleaners."

He laughed. "Well, you've come to the right place. If you were selling booze and dice, though, you'd really make a killin'. Come in and sit down. I think we need to talk."

Anderson looked as well-scrubbed as I had remembered him. He was still burly, too. But despite his large, dominating size there was a childlike quality about him, like he was ready to burst out with laughter at any moment.

"Ross, it's good to see you," he said, motioning for me

to sit in his desk chair while he sat on the edge of his bunk. "Is your family here?"

"Yeah, we've found an apartment in Melrose Park," I said. "We just arrived from San Diego. I sure wish I was back there, instead of here."

"Don't you like the cold weather?" He smiled. "I kind of enjoy it, myself."

"It's not the weather, Roger. It's the duty station. I really feel like I've been put out to pasture. I've never seen a more disgraceful ship."

Anderson nodded. I could see the negative talk struck a chord in him.

"I'd hoped you'd be a little more reassuring, Ross," he said. "But I can see you feel about the same way I do." He dropped his head and looked at his hands, toying with his naval academy ring.

"I don't understand what these orders are about. I've kept my nose clean. It's as if the navy just threw a bunch of names in a hat and picked out mine—and yours," he added with a sour grin. "Imagine two academy graduates on a naval reserve training ship. And we're due to have another Annapolis grad arrive any day."

"Well, I don't know about you, Roger, but this has just about caused me to forget any ideas I had about a navy career," I said bitterly.

"I'm sorry to hear that, Ross," he sympathized. "I haven't really made up my mind yet. I'd like to hang in there and try to transfer to the West Coast; my wife loves it out there."

"Yeah, so do we."

"Whaddya know about the captain?" he asked out of the blue. "I know this much myself: This is his first shipboard command. He's navy reserve now, but he served some time in the regular navy. I'm not sure where."

The young lieutenant left his bunk and walked to his

locker, where he began changing out of his uniform into civilian clothes. "You don't have a watch tonight, do you? How about some dinner?" he asked. "There's a little Italian place in town that has great food . . . and a nice little bar."

"No, I think I'll go on home," I said. "Listen, where can I find a cabin that doesn't look like a cyclone's hit it?"

"I'm afraid they're all like that. You can take your pick."

"I was afraid you'd say that," I said with a weak smile. "Good seeing ya, Roger." I closed the door behind me and walked to the next cabin.

Rather than offer me the solace I needed, my conversation with Lieutenant Anderson caused me to feel even more distressed. And the dreaded chore of cleaning up my cabin still remained. But first I wanted to call Pat.

Exiting the ship, I walked quickly to the nearest phone booth and dialed.

"Ross! Hi, hon. I was waiting for you to call. Is everything OK?"

"Yeah," I said. "It's going to be a little while yet before I'm settled."

"Is the ship what you expected?"

"Worse," I said. "It's the worst I've ever seen. And the crew is something else. But I got here OK."

"Oh, Ross," she said sympathetically.

"Yeah, but the navy plans to overhaul it, so the executive officer says. To modernize it," I added sarcastically. "But there's nothing it can do about the crew. I've never seen a less disciplined bunch.

"Imagine being responsible for the gunnery department. Gunnery on a destroyer escort is dangerous even with a good, disciplined crew."

"You sound pretty blue. Will you be OK?"

"Yeah, I guess so," I replied. "I'm just dreading

cleaning up my cabin. It's a real mess. I've got to have things ready for our little cruise tomorrow. We're going out on Lake Michigan."

"Well, I'll let you go then. I'll have dinner ready for you when you get home. . . . And Ross? The Lord will see us through this time. Just try to relax. I love you."

"OK. Love you, too. Bye."

I didn't want to concern Pat any further, but I was frankly afraid to relax. On this ship I felt more pressure than I'd ever felt before in the navy. As the ship's gunnery officer, it was obvious I would play a large part in the ship's command. I shuddered to think of the relationship I was bound to have with these untrained, unserious men, especially knowing how perfectionistic I was—when it came to a ship's guns and on-board ammunition. I had visions of shells being dropped and guns being mishandled, which could send someone to the hospital or all one hundred and ninety of us up in a cloud of smoke.

I'm going to be a real bear to live with, I thought. *I hope I'll be able to loosen up and not be so tense. Thank the Lord there isn't a speck of chance we'd ever be thrust into a combat situation. We'd never get out of it alive.*

The following weekend the captain, Comdr. Robert Phelps, called me to his office. I'd only briefly spoken to him during the training cruise last Saturday. He was pleasant enough, but I detected a never-say-die attitude about him; it was as if he was apt at any moment to do something outlandish and dare you to question him about it.

I sensed immediately that he'd called me to his cabin to discuss the orders he'd been expecting.

He had a slight gleam in his eye as he spoke, like he'd just pulled off the biggest ruse in the history of the navy.

"Mr. Campbell, we've received orders to head out the

Saint Lawrence Seaway to the Atlantic," he announced dramatically.

He sat proudly back in his chair, waiting to view my reaction.

"Out to the Atlantic?" I tried to speak calmly and hide my surprise. "For what reason?"

"Well, I don't really know the answer to that." His manner was almost arrogant. "But we're figuring into the navy's present alert, apparently. President Kennedy's calling up more reserves all the time because of this Berlin thing and the Soviets' aggressive actions."

"Are we going into dry dock on the East Coast?" I asked.

"I don't know, Lieutenant. But that's my guess."

I was flabbergasted. We could be in dry dock for months. That would mean pulling up stakes and relocating Pat and Carey wherever I was on the East Coast, because I wasn't about to leave them alone in the heart of Chicago.

"Any idea how long we'll be in dry dock?" I asked. "I mean, what has to be done?"

"A lot," he stated abruptly. "We'll have to upgrade the ship's sonar and radar, install new communications gear, and overhaul the guns and engines, at least."

"So when do we get underway?" I asked.

"Next Wednesday, if all goes according to plan," he said. "We'll have to inform the men of this extended tour of duty and make the necessary preparations with engineering.

"And," he paused, "after talking to the executive officer, I've decided that you're also going to be our communications officer from here on. We'd expected one on board, but it didn't happen."

The news caught me off guard.

"It'll be hard on you to handle communications and gunnery," he continued, "but there's no choice. Sorry."

"I appreciate your faith in me, sir," I managed to say. "I've never served in that capacity before. I'm not familiar at all with the equipment."

He produced a booklet from his desk and threw it at me.

"Here," he said, "bone up with this. And you'll need to go to supply at Great Lakes and get us some phones. The communications in the seaway are civilian. You'll need to be aware of that. OK?" A broad grin spread across his round face.

"Yes, sir," I replied. I nodded slowly and half smiled. The booklet in my hands was tattered, and looked to be nearly as old as I. "I'll do the best I can."

I had to call Pat immediately with the news. We'd been heartbroken upon learning of our transfer to Chicago, and now after only two months and a reasonably settled routine, it looked as if we'd be on the move again. But to where?

Pat tried to remain calm on the telephone, but at home later that night it was evident she was upset. The idea of having me head off to points unknown, while she and Carey faced fending for themselves in strange surroundings, was a cold and cruel development.

"When will we know something definite?" she asked.

"I'm surprised we don't know now," I said. "I'm really baffled by all of this. From what I could gather, the captain apparently has the orders, but he's not permitted to open them until we're in the Atlantic."

"Well," Pat said, sighing, "that's crazy. I guess that's the navy for you."

I fought against voicing any of my negative feelings for Pat's sake, knowing that her disappointment was as great as my own. Considering the arbitrary manner in which our lives had been pulled and twisted like leaves in the wind these past few months made me angrier by the minute. But I was helpless to do anything but wait out the mysterious new orders for my misfit ship.

"Things will work out, Ross," Pat forced herself to say. "I know they will. You'll get a nice port on the East Coast, someplace we've never seen before. It'll be all right. I'm praying everything will be all right."

"Yeah, it will," I sighed. "But listen, I want you to call your aunt immediately and see if they can put you up while I'm gone. I don't want you and Carey staying here alone."

"Well, OK. That's a good idea."

"I'll have the navy pick up our furniture and store it until I know where we're going," I said.

Pat's eyes looked grave. She appeared more glum than I'd ever known her. Seeing her like this only added to my disappointment.

The fear that we might be placed on alert and ordered to steam toward a tense coastal area in another part of the world rippled through me. *I can't let anything destroy what I have with my family. I can't.*

The fact that the USS *Daniel A. Joy* appeared so dispensible to the navy kept resurfacing in my thoughts as the days drew closer for our departure. *The navy could afford to lose such an ignoble ship,* I mulled darkly. *But we'd be a laughing stock in combat. . . . The navy wouldn't dare. Not if they knew anything about this crew. They wouldn't dare. . . .*

In a week's time, the eve of the ship's planned passage through the seaway had arrived. I'd just finished having dinner and was sitting in the wardroom, about to go on watch, when Roger Anderson walked up. We'd both been so busy doing administrative work and assigning duties to the men in our respective divisions that we'd hardly seen each other.

He immediately joined me. We spent some time talking about our families, until the conversation turned to the ship's upcoming movement on the seaway.

As the *Joy's* engineering officer, Roger was far more

informed than I about the ship's condition and its future overhaul. But as to where we were headed, he could only speculate like the rest of us.

He guessed the ship was destined for Newport, Rhode Island—the headquarters of the Atlantic destroyer fleet—and that we'd spend a relatively brief time, perhaps six weeks, in dry dock undergoing modernization.

"A real rush job—that's my guess, Ross," he said. "We're no good to the navy if we stay in dry dock. We wouldn't be going in for a complete overhaul with this alert the president's called."

"Will we be going back to Chicago, then?"

"I don't know," he replied with a shake of his head. "I doubt it."

"Things are tense in Europe. I wouldn't think the navy'd send us out on alert, but I'm always three steps behind those guys in Washington."

"Yeah, aren't we all?"

As the conversation continued, Roger said he'd been able to gather what he knew about the ship's future movements from the talk going around the message center.

"I just put two and two together," he said. "Hey, you're the new communcations officer," he added, chuckling, "put in a call to Washington."

I ignored his joke and sat back. "Why are we being kept in the dark about all of this?"

"You know we're not going to get any respect on a reserve training ship," he said indignantly. "The navy would rather keep our crew in the dark than have a lot of talk about any upcoming exercises."

"Well, I want to bring my family to our next port, if we're going to stay on the East Coast," I commented. "I wish we knew where we were going."

"I don't think even the captain knows yet."

I'd said my good-byes to Pat and Carey on the telephone
the night before. We were due to get underway by 0800,
which forced me to remain on board overnight. After a
fitful night's sleep, I rose about sunrise and climbed to
the main deck.

Gusty early fall winds tugged at my uniform and
whipped the ship's flag. The morning sky was
completely cloudless, permitting me an unobstructed
view of the golden sun as it rose over a still slumbering
downtown Chicago beyond the autumn-colored banks of
Lake Michigan.

Several hundred miles further east in Ohio, Carey and
Pat were no doubt still asleep. I felt guilty, as though it
were truly my fault for abandoning them like this. When
I'd be able to return and try to make it all up to them
was an answer no one seemed able to give.

Why, Lord, does life have to be so hard? I prayed
silently. *Your hand's in everything, I know, but
sometimes you seem so far away.*

At slightly past 0800, the ship began its swing out into
the still expanse of Lake Michigan. Other nearby vessels,
dwarfed by this fossil ship, bobbed in the *Joy's* wake.
The familiar metallic noises coming from our engine
rooms were like the groans of some half-awake creature
rising from slumber. And I was in the creature's chest,
fumbling to make contact with civilian communicators
in the narrow straits of the Saint Lawrence Seaway ahead.

Here we come, world, I thought. *Look out.*

After roughly two days of cruising north through Lake
Michigan and then into Lake Erie, we reached the
seaway. It soon became apparent just how treacherous
the body of water could be. A navy vessel, we'd been
told, had never before attempted passage through the
Great Lakes to the Atlantic, and I could see why:
Numerous locks presented those of us on the bridge

with a new challenge around virtually every bend.

This is an extremely difficult passage, it dawned on me. *That's the reason for the arrival of regular navy officers. Maybe the navy had some respect for our abilities after all. And maybe once we're on the East Coast, I'll be finished with this duty station.*

I shut off my wishful thinking and turned back to my communication and gunnery duties. I didn't want to get my hopes up.

➧ *I will make darkness light before them, and crooked things straight* (Isa. 42:16, KJV).

➧ *When a door slams behind you, look for the one God is opening* (Eleanor Doan).

CHAPTER

ON THE BRINK OF
WORLD WAR III

A violent shake startled me out of the peaceful sanctuary
of my slumber. From out of nowhere a big arm had
appeared, jerked back the drapes of my berth, and
grabbed my shoulder.

"I'm awake! I'm awake!" I responded, annoyed at such
a rough intrusion.

It was just past 1300 hours (1:00 P.M.), according to
my wristwatch. I felt as if I'd only been resting for ten
minutes, but in fact, forty-five minutes had passed since I
lay down.

"Captain wants to see ya, Lieutenant." The young sailor
stared down at me to see if I'd heard him. I could
plainly see him squinting at me through the darkness of
my cabin. The big blond, whom everyone called Tex,
obviously did not see I was looking right at him.

I lay there trying to clear the cobwebs, not yet having

the strength to speak or the energy to swing my feet over onto the shifting deck.

"Did ya hear me?" He pressed his face forward almost until it was touching mine, darting his head in circles to determine whether my eyes were open or closed. He pulled back when I blinked.

"Yes, I hear you. And I'm getting up." I took several deep breaths, trying to relieve the pressure in my head and stomach. "Tell the captain I'm on my way."

I thought I had my sea legs, but I quickly learned differently early in the day. The passage through the seaway had taken almost ten days. No sooner had we reached the Atlantic than I got that old, familiar "green-gilled" feeling. I couldn't remember ever feeling so sick. What made my seasickness even harder to swallow was that no one else—not even one of these greenhorns—seemed to be suffering as much as me.

I guessed the candy bar I had eaten for breakfast while I was on watch had done it.

The ship had left the mouth of the Saint Lawrence Seaway roughly two hours earlier, and been caught almost immediately in an off-coast storm. I was forced to leave my post at the bridge after watch and make for the nearest head and then my bunk, as the ship's pitch and yaw had steadily grown more violent.

The storm was still raging as I stood up in my cabin. I breathed deeply several times in an effort to neutralize my nausea, but the ship's constant rocking motion allowed me no reprieve. Putting on my shoes and shirt took every bit of strength I had.

I shakily made my return to the bridge, bracing myself against the bulkheads with each onslaught of high waves. The storm seemed to be growing even greater in intensity. I feared the ship might capsize.

"I hope he has good reasons for putting me through this," I muttered. I suspected the captain was summoning me back to the bridge to inform me of our new orders. If that was the case, we'd have to set up a new communications network.

Commander Phelps was looking for me, and he saw me step onto the bridge. He turned his eyes back to his work after spotting me.

"You OK, Ross?" he chuckled. "Pretty rough out here, huh?"

I detected a bit of sarcasm in his voice, but my annoyance faded when he gave me a look of fatherly concern and then smiled. The presence of several buckets on the bridge told me few were being spared the intestinal torment I was experiencing. But no one, I concluded, seemed to be doing any worse than me, the Annapolis grad, Mr. Regular Navy—a point that the reserve commander appeared to enjoy.

"Yes, sir, it is rough," I said. I wiped the cold sweat from my brow with my shirtsleeve. "This is the worst storm I've seen."

"Awww, we'll make it through." I had to smile at this display of bravado that was probably being made at my expense. A kid with a new toy wouldn't be more excited than this first-time captain.

Let him enjoy his fun, I thought. *But, Lord, don't let him dump us in the drink.*

Within a half hour, the storm began to subside, and I felt some color coming back to my pale cheeks. Commander Phelps left the captain's chair and walked over to me.

"We're going to Newport, Ross," he said quietly. "Goin' into dry dock. You feel up to raising a signal for us, and lettin' them know we're comin'?"

"Yes, sir. I'm feeling much better."

Just as I'd guessed, the captain had gotten permission to open our secret orders. "For how long, sir?" I asked.

"Not sure. Six weeks, maybe more." He seemed to

have read my mind and answered my next question. "Dunno where we're headed for next," he said. "Most of the destroyer fleet's already out on alert, though."

Newport. That's just great, I thought. *I'll have to move Pat and Carey all the way to the East Coast after all.*

I longed for my family. I agonized to think we'd have to relocate again. Adding to my chagrin was the looming possibility that we'd eventually be placed on alert after being overhauled. I certainly hoped the tension would pass before our time in dry dock was up.

If the alert was not lifted, however, I knew I'd have few sympathizers. Despite the momentary discomfort, nearly all of these reservists were already bright-eyed and passionately enjoying their first taste of the sea. To go on alert and steam toward some trouble spot in the world would make them absolutely delirious.

Three days later, about 1600 (4:00 P.M.), we reached the Rhode Island coast. We arrived at Newport around 1735 hours, and moored securely at the navy pier shortly thereafter. We'd depart tomorrow for dry dock further down the channel.

It was overcast and cold, but the large naval installation was teeming with activity when I finally got off the ship. The people milling around the commissary were mostly young sailors and navy wives and their children—indicative, it seemed to me, of the alert, which had brought out the reserves and taken regular navy men away from their families.

I quickly located a phone and called Pat in Ohio.

Her aunt answered the phone. "Ross, where are you?" she inquired.

"We're in Newport, Rhode Island."

"Newport. Well, that's a nice town, I hear. It's so good to hear from you. Did you have a good trip?"

I knew she didn't really want to hear what I had to say about my trip.

"Yes, it was fine," I replied, trying to be accommodating. "Everything's fine."

Finally, Pat and Carey took the line. It was good to hear their voices after the coarse gutter language and silly laughter I'd been subjected to for the better part of two weeks.

I talked to the two of them for a good thirty minutes, with the earpiece pressed hard to my ear to hear over the navy yard noise.

"How soon do you think you can find us a place to stay?" Pat asked. "And when can you get away? We're ready to leave as soon as you get here."

"Tomorrow's Saturday," I said. "I can get a three-day leave and fly over. I'll let you know when. Probably Sunday or Monday."

In less than four days, I managed to rent a nice little house in an attractive neighborhood, fly back to Ohio, load up our belongings, and drive back with Pat and Carey. We stayed in a Newport motel for two nights as we awaited the arrival of our furniture.

I was happy to have my wife and daughter with me, but I could not break the gloom stemming from the uncertainty I felt over my future. Each day, I tried to pick up bits and pieces of information by talking to people around the base and aboard the ship to find out where we were headed next.

One day Roger Anderson called me to his cabin. I figured he had gotten some inside information. I wasn't expecting the double shock he threw at me.

"Ross, the ship is going to Guantánamo Bay, Cuba," he said. "That's the latest news from the message center."

I was floored. "Oh, come on, Roger," I said, slapping my legs in exasperation, "you're not serious." Gitmo is the gloomiest naval base in the world.

"Yes. And it looks as if we'll be the only regular navy officers left on board. Lieutenant Smith is getting a transfer."

I leaned back and ran both hands through my hair. "I guess we're just the goats of the bunch," I complained. "Who's going to be the executive officer?"

"I guess you are," he said.

Roger tried to be upbeat. "The way I figure it, Ross, the ship will probably make one sweep down there, and we'll spend a short time in Newport. We'll certainly be given a duty station we want after that."

"I intend to finish up my hitch and resign my commission," I said bluntly. "I've thought a lot about it. I might even enter medical school."

"Med school, huh," he said, nodding. "If that's what you want. I want to get orders to the West Coast. I figure I'll hang in there."

Roger had to go on watch, so we terminated our conversation. I thanked him for the information. "Warn me the next time you have some info, OK?"

So now the crew was down to one hundred two enlisted men, ten reserve officers, including the commander, and Roger and me, the USS *Daniel A. Joy's* sole surviving regular navy officers.

And the navy was sending us in the company of an almost brand-new, modern destroyer fleet on the East Coast.

I spent the day prior to our departure for Cuba at home with Pat and Carey saying my good-byes. I made no attempts to try and cover my disappointment. But as usual, Pat sought to keep the conversation light and positive. Her outlook was actually making it all the more difficult to leave: She was the best cheerleader a man could have.

Saying good-bye was especially hard in light of the heightening tensions between the Soviet Union and the United States, which made our movement to Cuba all the more grave. An alert that included the reserves and National Guard had not been imposed by the president since the Korean War.

Plus, I felt an enormous amount of remorse in having to practically dump Pat and Carey in a New England town that was totally foreign to them. They would be here alone in the middle of winter, without relatives or friends to help them get acclimated. I wished I'd left them in Ohio.

I was pleased that Pat had made arrangements weeks before to spend Christmas in Florida with her folks. I was happy for them, but it didn't brighten my outlook on having to spend my holiday on board the *Joy.*

To walk out of our house on the evening before my departure, with Pat and Carey waving at the front door, took every bit of strength I had. "Bye, Daddy," Carey called as I opened the door of the cab that would take me to the ship. "We'll have Christmas for you when you get back," Pat said.

Inside the cab, alone with my misery, I looked back on my navy career and the decisions that had brought me to this point. I hadn't bargained for any of this when I sought entrance into Annapolis. True to my nature, I saw the navy as having delivered me with slap after cold slap in the face since entering the academy. God's presence was all that could remove this darkness hanging over me.

I quoted a favorite Scripture to myself as I rode: "God is our refuge and strength, a very present help in trouble. Therefore will not we fear, though the earth be removed, and though the mountains be carried into the midst of the sea; though the waters thereof roar and be troubled, though the mountains shake with the swelling thereof."

After several repeatings, the forty-sixth Psalm gave me the assurance and hope I sought. God spoke directly to me through the passage, as he had on other occasions. My current situation looked pretty bleak, but I shuddered to think how I would face life without God and his abiding grace.

In the artificial gleam of the dock lights the ship looked virtually the same; there were still some chipped, peeling spots on the outer bulkheads that the paint-brushes had missed. But it was ready, so we were told. The engines had been refitted, and the pre-World War II sonar and radar equipment upgraded. The guns had been overhauled, too. To think they would ever be needed sent cold shivers up my spine.

Reports of our upcoming duties were sketchy, but from what I could gather we would be homeported at Guantánamo Bay and patroling the Windward Straits between Cuba and Jamaica on a rotating basis with the other ships in our reserve squadron.

Any foreign ships entering the straits would be stopped and searched. It was no secret to anyone that the navy's move to launch such an operation was precipitated by the increase of Russian merchant shipping in the region and the threat of nuclear missiles being sent to Cuba.

I had learned that eight other reserve ships, most of which were in even worse condition than the *Joy,* would make up our squadron, Cortron-8. How vital any of the ships had been in their better days, I did not know, but one thing was certain: No escort fleet of destroyers in the history of the U.S. Navy had ever been sent on a more crucial mission any more ill-prepared.

On November 8, 1961, at 1037 hours my ship, the USS *Daniel A. Joy,* and the rest of the ships in our escort, left the coast of Rhode Island without fanfare on the dreariest of autumn days.

Shortly thereafter we passed unscathed through the treacherous waters of Cape Hatteras—usually a sailor's nightmare due to its rough conditions.

My seasickness was considerably more tolerable than it had been on our maiden Atlantic voyage, but it began to dawn on me just how poor my physical condition was. I felt myself becoming weaker as my body fought against every yaw and pitch on this tiny tin can.

In forty-eight hours, we were still roughly a week away from the base at Guantánamo. As we steamed farther south, warmer temperatures stoked by the Caribbean trade winds created a flurry of excitement among the crew members, most of whom hailed from the now frozen Midwest. The prospect of basking in the hot sun, downing bottles of rum, and chasing flowered skirts in the middle of December was simply beyond their wildest dreams. It didn't seem to matter to them that Guantánamo Bay, Cuba, had the unsavory nickname, the Hole.

Either to celebrate their upcoming "vacation" in the Caribbean or merely to herald our arrival, several of the more slaphappy members of the crew prepared a little surprise just prior to arriving at our destination.

I was in my cabin doing paperwork when I heard the clamor of men running to the main deck to get a look at "the black cloud."

Howls of laughter and screams of "Whew, what a smell!" and "I can't believe they did it!" brought me out of my quarters to see what all the excitement was about.

From a hatchway near the bridge I could see a huge column of smoke pouring from the ship's smokestacks and trailing for a hundred or more yards behind us.

The bridge was practically filled with the swirling black smoke when I arrived. It had the familiar stench of burning oil.

The commander was in a state of panic, calling the engineering and fire watch crews on two separate phones to investigate the cause of the smoke.

"It's not a fire, it's a prank, Captain!" I yelled. "Someone is pulling a prank!" The captain stopped in midstride and spun toward me.

"Well, who in the h——— would do a thing like this?" he shouted between coughs. I explained that from what

I could gather, someone had dumped a chemical mixture into the ship's steam engine. "It's probably mostly oil, Captain."

He fanned his hands to clear the air. I could see he was embarrassed and perturbed. "These idiots. They'll try just about anything." The captain glanced at me to view my expression. I was smiling, trying desperately not to laugh.

"But d--- it, this shouldn't have happened." He looked a little frustrated, like a scoutmaster who'd let his boys get carried away with their fun and games. "A stunt like this could ruin the ship's engines."

He turned toward me in the black cloud. "Lieutenant, call the engineering officer and tell him to inform his men that under no circumstances is anyone to ever pull a trick like this again."

"Aye, aye, Sir."

The black cloud never appeared again, and no one ever revealed the identity of the perpetrator, who was dubbed The Shadow.

With the exception of the black cloud, things progressed routinely as we slowly chugged toward the southeastern end of Cuba. In fact, I was miserably bored.

What proved to be a saving grace for me during this period of boredom and disgruntlement was the continued zaniness of the crew. As I got to know some of them, I realized that the constant stream of jokes and kidding was their way of making things tolerable.

I learned to appreciate many of the men personally, despite their continued irreverence regarding serious shipboard duties and restrictions. And I sensed their affection and esteem for me growing as well, as I loosened up and settled into my role on the crew.

As for the effect of my Christianity, I was pleased that no one really held my faith in great contempt, but neither was I packing them in at the Sunday morning services I conducted in the mess hall.

The lull in my duties at sea allowed me to do a lot of witnessing to the men and the officers, which kept up my spirits somewhat. I managed to win two enlisted men to Christ on the way down to Cuba, and took great delight in watching them grow in the Lord.

The gap between my values and those of many of the other men was no better demonstrated than when a projector and a stack of X-rated stag films would be produced. Without knowing what the night's feature was, I was sitting calmly one night, anticipating the entertainment, when suddenly some highly arousing sexual scenes filled the screen. The provocative nature of the film was simply too much for me to take, and I had to leave the wardroom.

The men seemed to get as much fun out of ribbing me as they did in viewing the films.

"What's the matter, Ross?" they hooted. "Having a hard time? Gettin' to ya?"

"Hang around," another voice yelled as I exited. "We haven't even gotten to the good parts yet."

I didn't stay the butt of their good-natured kidding very long, however. Indeed, I was probably the most indispensable member of the ship's crew, sometimes to my frustration.

I was only a lieutenant, junior grade, but because I was regular navy I enjoyed greater influence with the captain than probably all of the reserve officers put together. The commander was cocky, but he did not make any major decisions without first consulting me.

I was dramatically made aware of this influence on a cloudless, balmy-winded afternoon less than twenty-four hours from our scheduled arrival in Guantánamo Bay.

At approximately 1600 hours, a jet fighter plane suddenly crashed in the Atlantic no more than four hundred yards from our ship. We heard first the tumultuous roar of the plane's malfunctioning engines, followed by a tremendous splash off our port side.

Buoyed by its cargo, the plane's wreckage remained partially afloat for several minutes before sinking. The crew was lost. All that remained of the wreckage were two large fuel tanks bobbing on the water's surface.

Without any apparent forethought or trepidation, the captain immediately instructed the ship's frogmen to suit up and swim to the tanks for the purpose of salvaging them.

When I eventually came on deck, I was horrified. The entire crew had stopped its work and was intently watching the progress of the frogmen.

After several minutes the swimmers arrived at the tanks. Those of us on ship soon noticed that the splashing of the frogmen had aroused the interest of a number of sharks. As many as ten or fifteen fins seemed to appear in the water at once.

To avert attack, the frogmen climbed up on the fuel tanks and straddled them like wet-suited cowboys in a water rodeo.

Suddenly, I detected the unmistakable sound of gunshots. When I saw tiny splashes in the water coinciding with the sound of the gunshots, I became absolutely horrified.

"Captain!" I hollered, racing to the bridge. "What's going on?"

He was enjoying the proceedings as one would a tennis match. The cheers and shouted instructions of the crew could be heard throughout the ship.

"Why, we're protectin' those men out there," he said indignantly. "Don't you see the sharks?"

"Forget the sharks!" I exclaimed. "Captain, you've got to stop the firing! If one of those shots hits a tank, those men are dead. There'll be an explosion like you've never seen."

He looked at me quizzically. "Yeah, I guess you're

right," he replied, the folly of his actions suddenly occurring to him.

"Cease firing!" The rescue personnel on the main deck relayed his command, and the men put down their rifles.

"Now what?" he asked in an almost childlike manner.

"First we need to get those men out of the water," I said. "Pull the ship alongside the wreckage. We'll pick up the divers, then retrieve the wreckage with the freight nets."

He gave the orders to do as I suggested.

It was satisfying to me professionally to have the ear of the ship's captain. But it frightened me to realize how poor his judgment was. I was afraid to let the man out of my sight. Fortunately, he never let me get too far away, anyway.

At last, after slightly less than ten days at sea, we could see the palm-lined beaches, cragged cliffs, and sloping mountains that formed Guantánamo Bay. As we glided into the bay, we sighted a host of American ships— mostly destroyers and amphibians—dotting the expansive inlet.

For me, the heady scene evoked recollections of navy footage taken during World War II in the Pacific. I hoped the comparison would go no further than that.

I expected the sight of all these American ships to create a more serious, subdued mood among the crew. Instead, they remained as restless as penned bulls, eager to sample all the delights this tropical region had to offer—and, to my horror, to "get into it" with whatever hostile forces we might encounter.

I certainly shared their anticipation of hitting dry land, although for vastly different reasons. I longed for a decent, hot meal and a hot shower, which was practically a luxury on ship due to a shortage of fresh water. The majority of the crew members, it was obvious, had other needs on their minds.

I'd never been to Guantánamo Bay, but I was convinced that anything it had to offer would be a welcome improvement to the ship's fares.

Lieutenant Smith had a strange look on his face as he approached me on the bridge just prior to our swing toward the navy docks. He seemed reluctant to say whatever it was he had on his mind.

"Uh, Ross," he finally said. "Uh, the captain asked me to appoint you head of shore patrol while we're here." Shore patrol is the navy's military police. It's responsible to keep the sailors out of trouble onshore.

I listened reluctantly. "Shore patrol?"

"Yes, Lieutenant. He figured you didn't have any plans of going out and, well, you know . . . getting drunk or anything." He gave a light laugh. "Somebody's got to stay sober."

"Just how long a duty are we talking about?" I asked.

"Over the weekend," he replied.

"The weekend?!" I came back.

"Well, Ross, you won't be the only one to do it," he consoled. "I'll make sure you're relieved. We just need someone like yourself to stay on top of things."

Our patrol of the Windward Straights was scheduled to begin on Monday. The captain informed the ship's officers that our orders were to intercept any foreign vessels and demand they disclose who they were and what cargo they carried. (I knew that the term *foreign* was another way of saying Russian.) The order to halt any vessels and board them would come from the captain.

Simple enough, I thought. *But what if a foreign ship chooses to ignore our demands?*

The tension in the region was keenly felt by both Cuban nationals and the American sailors and marines stationed in the area. Within hours after the arrival of our squadron in "Gitmo," as we called it, the navy's defense perimeter had been ordered strengthened to hold off any possible attack by Castro.

In April earlier in the year, Cuban rebels had unsuccessfully stormed their homeland in an effort to overthrow the Communist-supported dictator Fidel Castro. There was no denying that the ill-fated Bay of Pigs invasion had left lingering animosity toward the U.S. on the part of many Cubans.

The aggressive action of the Soviets just months before to block further movement of Germans from Communist East Germany to democratic West Germany would seem to have little effect on this remote Caribbean location. But Cuba was a hotbed for Communism. If the U.S. military alert was critical for assuaging Communist hostility elsewhere in the world, it had to apply here as well.

But the captain didn't let the important business of patroling spoil his fun. At the end of our final pass on patrol before heading back to Guantánamo Bay, the captain would radio a message to the base that the ship was experiencing engine trouble. Conveniently, this reported malfunctioning of the ship's engines always managed to occur near Jamaica.

Once landing at the Kingston pier, the men would tear off, ready to taste its luscious, not-at-all-forbidden fruits. That is, everyone except me; I would don my shore patrol gear and hit the docks.

While I was on shore patrol during one such Jamaican port call, the captain roared up in a beautiful silver Cadillac driven by an equally beautiful girl. Her long, brown tresses spilled luxuriously over her shoulders. Two attractive blonds adorned the sleek automobile's back seat.

He was wearing the loudest Hawaiian shirt I'd ever seen.

"Hey, Ross," he hollered giddily. "You got ten bucks I can borrow?"

I couldn't believe my eyes and ears. This was the captain of a U.S. Navy ship? He looked more like a conventioneer in Hawaii suffering from a terminal case of seven-year-itch. And imagine—him borrowing money from me.

I reached in my pocket for my wallet and gave him ten dollars.

"Thanks, Ross," he slurred as I handed him the bill. "See ya back on the ship." The silky-haired, well-tanned driver wheeled the car in the gravel and the four of them sped away from the docks.

I thought about what had just transpired, and wondered why on earth the captain would borrow a mere ten dollars when he was surrounded by three seemingly well-heeled women.

I toyed for a moment with the possibilities and shrugged my shoulders. Why should I expect anything or anyone associated with the ship to make sense now?

The following day the crew was uncharacteristically subdued. We were due to get back on patrol, and that meant leaving the sunny Jamaican paradise. The hangovers plaguing most of the men didn't brighten the chores awaiting them on ship.

The general cheerlessness of the crew pervaded the wardroom at dinner that night. Adding to everyone's discomfort was a devastating heat wave that made the conditions on board utterly miserable.

A few days later at dinner, the captain plopped down in his chair and began filling his plate. Suddenly, he snapped his fingers. "Oh, Ross," he said, looking up. He reached in his pocket. "Here's the ten bucks I owe ya."

His brazenness took me by surprise. "Uh, thanks," I said. As a result of my embarrassment, I knocked over the pitcher of milk, spilling it over more than half of the table. I was so unnerved, I stood up.

"Now for my next trick," I quipped. The entire table broke up in laughter.

"Ross, you're something else," the captain said,

laughing. "I don't know what we'd do without you."

The next day was hardly one for being jovial. The searing Caribbean sun made even the ship's outer bulkheads nearly impossible to touch. Everyone spent the morning in the same manner we had spent the last two: trying to stay cool. And why not? We hadn't seen a single ship on patrol.

Then without warning, the crew was jolted out of its heat-induced stupor by the alarm for general quarters. A loud voice followed over the intercom.

"All hands report to battle stations. Unidentified vessel sighted."

As gunnery officer, I scrambled from my cabin to my assigned battle station on the bridge. Sure enough, at ten o'clock, off our port side, an unfamiliar ship was proceeding right down our assigned corridor.

"It's a Russian ship disguised as a freighter," the captain said solemnly. "It's heavily armed, too. I wonder what they're up to?"

In no time the ship was in close enough range to read its markings. It was a Russian vessel, and its sizable cargo was easily identified as land-to-land missles.

"Send the signal, quartermaster, requesting that they identify themselves," the captain called out. A somber, almost grim pall had fallen over the bridge.

The quartermaster stepped to his position behind the signal flasher and sent the message in international code. Several minutes passed with no reply.

The captain looked intensely at the ship and then at the quartermaster. In another moment, the captain walked a short distance across the bridge to the quartermaster's station.

"Send it again," he said.

For a minute there was no reply, and then the Russian ship's signal lamp began flashing slowly.

When the flashing had ended, the quartermaster turned. He had a sickened look on his face.

"Well?" the captain barked. "What did they say?"

The sailor's hands were trembling where they rested on the flasher handles. "They said, 'None of your g—— d——— business.' "

"That's what they said?!" the captain shouted indignantly. "I'll tell them whose business it is! I know who they are! They just don't realize who they're playing with!"

Commander Phelps stormed away from the quartermaster, slamming his foot down hard as he stepped through a hatchway back onto the bridge.

"Send a message demanding that they reveal what it is they're carrying as cargo!" he hollered over his shoulder. "I wanna know what they say to this."

The quartermaster flashed out the message. The response was a short burst of flashes.

"Well, what did they say?" the captain asked.

"Uh, I think they said, 'S———.' "

"What!?" he roared.

"S———, sir."

"I heard you! I heard you!"

Commander Phelps became absolutely livid. He stood with his hands on his hips staring at the Russian vessel, which in the meantime had increased its speed.

"All engines ahead, flank!"

In several minutes' time, the Russian ship had begun edging away from us. Our ship's relatively outdated engines, which were capable of no more than eighteen knots tops, were obviously no match for the new Russian vessel, which had the capability of doing at least thirty knots. As it was, with our ship's limited range of radar and sonar, we had been little more than sitting ducks since our arrival in the Caribbean.

The captain stood frozen, deliberating what to do next. Adding to his frustration was the fact that the Russian ship had nearly passed us. Shortly, we were dead astern of them, looking at their fantail as we cruised in their wake.

In another moment, several Russian sailors appeared on the fantail, laughing hysterically as they threw boxes of garbage overboard directly into our path. When the captain realized what was happening, his eyes glazed and narrowed in rage.

"Ross!" he shouted, turning abruptly to me. "Load the guns!"

"Load the guns?!" I shouted in disbelief.

"And order them trained on the Russian vessel."

I stepped up to the captain.

"You don't intend to fire on them, do you?" I asked excitedly. "We don't have the authority to fire on them or any other ship."

The commander stood rigid, his hands on his hips. His pouting expression resembled that of a child intent on getting his way.

"Captain, we're looking at World War III here if we fire on a Russian merchant ship," I said in a low voice. "I don't care what they're carrying or how belligerent they intend to be, we're making a big mistake if we fire on that ship."

"Campbell," he barked, glaring at me, "I've given the order, and I'm the captain aboard this ship. I suggest you carry it out or risk court-martial. You'll just have to stand back and wait like the rest of us to see what happens."

This had been the only advice I'd ever given the captain that he hadn't taken wholeheartedly. Why did he have to be so single-minded now?

"Oh, God," I said as I reached for the phone to relay the order to my division.

"All mounts load. All directors train on the ship off the bow," I said.

I wanted to sink to my knees and pray. My heart was thumping madly in my chest. I looked around the bridge. Everyone was stricken with fear. I'd never seen a more petrified-looking group of men.

A minute passed. Then two minutes. At last a full five

minutes had passed. I felt like the captain might be bluffing, but I wasn't sure. I wondered if he was aware that all of civilization was at stake in this game of chicken he was playing with the Russians. And would he be foolish enough to give me the command, "Commence firing"?

I was gripped by the notion that I was watching history unfold. I prayed that God would permit cooler heads to prevail on the Russian ship, because I was standing next to a naval reserve captain who appeared determined to have it out, for whatever reason. Fortunately, they hadn't gotten so far ahead that they couldn't see our guns were loaded and aiming at them.

Several more minutes passed. Then, the Russian ship slowed drastically. In seconds, the message flasher aboard the Soviet vessel sent the information requested by the captain.

"They're a Soviet vessel," the quartermaster said. "They say they're carrying medical supplies, food, and hardware to Cuba."

The captain let out a little snort. "Yeah, and if anybody believes that, I have some prime real estate along the Cuban shoreline I'd like to sell.

"Well, we did our job," he said flatly. He surveyed the bridge slowly, showing off his satisfied look. "Unload all guns. All directors amidships," he ordered.

I was joined by everyone on the bridge in breathing a huge sigh of relief. My knees remained weak for the rest of the day.

In less than three weeks, the *Joy* steamed back to Newport. In another three weeks, I was practically jerked from the arms of my thankful family for the ship's passage back to Chicago, but this time I didn't mind. Chicago would actually look good to me.

Unbeknownst to us, Mayor Richard Daley and the city

of Chicago were poised to give the crew a hero's
welcome it would never forget.

The festivities began as soon as we landed at the docks
of the naval armory on a sunny July afternoon, almost
nine months to the day we sailed for Newport.

The headlines in the *Tribune* on the day of our arrival
read: "Chicago Welcomes Reservists—Autumn, Tears . . .
Today, *Joy!*"

I didn't feel like I deserved the title of hero; the
participation of the ship as a whole in the Berlin crisis
alert certainly wasn't what I'd term particularly heroic.
Nevertheless, I found it hard not to bask in the adulation
and good wishes heaped upon us.

The crew was whisked off the ship and carried around
Chicago in an open-car parade before being taken back
to the armory. There we were guests of honor at a
luncheon hosted by Mayor Daley and heads of the area's
naval commands.

My family set up residence once more in Chicago. Pat
and her sister had found a place for us to live shortly
before the ship's return. In Chicago I waited out the
remaining twelve months of my navy career and saw the
birth of our second child, Cathy.

The *Joy's* involvement during the Berlin crisis was
always a favorite topic when relatives or neighbors
would call. I was amused that the same ship that had
laughingly been referred to as "The Pride of Chicago"
and literally yanked out of mothballs for service should
come to be cherished as a city treasure.

That I had found myself an onlooker of history and
been feted in a hero's welcome as a result of orders that
initially appeared so dismal was equally ironic.

As with any experience fraught with toil and
disappointment, it was hard to find the hidden benefits
of my service aboard the *Joy.* Only much later did I
realize the storehouse of lessons about human nature and

God's dominion that my experience afforded me. Many of them still aid me to this day.

▶ *God is our refuge and strength, a very present help in trouble* (Ps. 46:1, KJV).

▶ *And I smiled to think God's greatness flowed around our incompleteness* . . . (Elizabeth Barrett Browning, "Rhyme of the Duchess May").

CHAPTER

SEEDS OF FAILURE

Looking back, I'm aware just how much my Christian faith was threatened during the latter part of my navy career and in the several years that followed. I was a classic example of the faltering middle-years Christian, as I've chosen to label it, because my feelings of depression and disillusionment were so overwhelming.

Only in retrospect can I see the extent of the spiritual paralysis I encountered during this period in my life. But God never kicked down the barriers I raised during this time of spiritual need. Instead, he remained steadfast until I recognized the importance of reopening the gates of my heart and relinquishing everything to him, including the hurts.

My commitment to witnessing and the practice of Christian meditation during my trying navy days let in the only real peace I had in the midst of my depression.

I couldn't exercise my body on board ship, which accounted for my poor physical condition during my naval career, so I spent as much time as possible guarding against spiritual atrophy. While I watered my spiritual garden, however, I should have checked to see whether I was standing on the hose, to borrow an analogy.

True, I was a victim of a bad set of circumstances in this period of my life. But as I've learned both firsthand and through the lives of my patients, we can often choose whether we'll be victims or victors.

My undoing during this time was my failure to aggressively trust in God's love and concern for me. Spiritual lethargy widened the gulf between myself and the Lord, who earnestly wanted to bless me and use me. As a result, I was ill-prepared for the singular blow that crippled my willingness to share the message of his salvation.

Only many years later did I learn just what God had been able to accomplish out of an incident I had written off as totally destructive.

At the outset, shore patrol on the streets of Guantánamo Bay had the prospect of being the least rewarding of my responsibilities. I had no inkling the duty would take on redeeming value when the three of us on patrol stumbled onto a Salvation Army service one night.

We arrived at the charity center just as the first people, most of whom were Cubans, began filing into the small room where the Salvation Army conducted its nightly meetings. I wondered if these impoverished people were truly interested in worship, or if their hunger and other needs had led them to this place.

A solitary ceiling fan whirled lazily from the ceiling. Those attending the service obviously weren't present to gain relief from the muggy heat: the fan only kept the hot air circulating evenly.

The fifty-odd chairs quickly filled up. At the front of the room stood a young, clean-cut man in shirtsleeves. A rickety lectern served as his pulpit on the makeshift wooden platform. Behind him hung a simple cross, fashioned, it appeared, out of the same wood that had been used for the platform and the lectern.

We stood at the back. Occasionally, the young Salvation Army official would look toward us and smile. He made his welcoming remarks both in Spanish and English, and delivered his short sermon in the same manner. He used several passages in James as the basis for his comments.

"We must count every difficulty as joy, as Saint Paul commanded," he began. "For times of temptation and trouble prove our faith. And faith increases our patience to withstand the next set of hardships."

He raised his arms to form a sphere. "It's a constant cycle. As we rejoice in difficulty, stronger becomes our faith and greater becomes our patience to withstand difficulty."

Next the young man urged his listeners to be Christians not only in word, but in deed. "The best witness is unspoken. Witness with what you are, not only with what you say. Your humility and long-suffering love spreads the kingdom of God—not your money, and certainly not your boasting."

He hoisted his Bible above his head. "God says the rich man and his money fade and wither like the scorched grass. God's people bear rich fruit and are given wealth of the spirit. These gifts will never fade."

After the service, the three of us greeted the young Salvation Army official.

"We enjoyed your message very much," I said. "It was good of you to deliver it in English, too."

He smiled broadly. "Well, I always try to accommodate American visitors and sailors. We don't get many of them here, though."

As the young missionary talked, we learned that the impoverished Cuban people did come to the center for more than the services. What little the Salvation Army had in food and clothing shipments from the United States was given to the poor.

When the three of us offered to bring extra food from the ship and donate it to the people, the young man grabbed each of our hands in appreciation.

"Thank you," he said. "I know God will bless anything you can bring us. What a wonderful witness it will be to our people."

"It will be our pleasure," said one of my companions.

"Maybe your generous act will help to mend some of the hostility the Cuban people feel toward the Americans. They don't trust the American military very much."

"I would guess that's true," I said. "I'm sorry that's a problem."

He suddenly laughed. "You're an answer to prayer, an answer to my sermon tonight. You'll help me in getting across my point about witness."

In a short time, the three of us began acquainting ourselves with the Salvation Army outposts in Guantánamo Bay and Jamaica. We laughingly called ourselves the Angels of Joy, because other than the two reservists on board I'd led to accept Christ, me and my two partners—both enlisted men—were the only other Christians on board.

It gave each of us a tremendous amount of satisfaction to be able to put the surplus food from the ship's galley to good use, rather than seeing it thrown in the garbage.

A lot of jokes are made about navy food. One sailor quipped, "You can take all of it if you want," when he realized what we were doing. But the Salvation Army officials were very appreciative to have something to give the hungry families and individuals who came for worship. We especially enjoyed seeing the looks on the peoples' faces when they found out where the food came from.

We always ran short of food—and time—at the Salvation Army centers, however. The call of duty to patrol the streets, back alleys, and beer joints was unfortunately a constant one.

The *Joy's* young reservists, some of whom were experiencing their first taste of being away from home, had to be watched like hawks. Obviously, you couldn't be everywhere at once, and invariably several times a night we would have to pull a young sailor to his feet through the trash and regurgitation and escort him back to the ship before he hurt himself or someone else.

Luckily, I could count on my shore patrol partners when the opportunity arose for me to attend meetings of the Officers' Christian Fellowship on base.

When I received the call on board ship inviting me to attend the Bible studies of the Guantánamo Bay chapter of OCF, I was absolutely overjoyed.

"How did you get my name?" I asked the caller, an ensign stationed at the base.

"From workers at the Salvation Army in town," he replied. "The help you gave them on shore patrol has been a real witness."

The ensign informed me that the meetings were held once a week. "When you're in port, we hope you can join us, Lieutenant."

"Listen, thanks a lot," I said. "I can really use the lift."

"I know exactly what you mean," he laughed. "I think the OCF meetings will be a real boost for you. We have some wonderful people attending."

True to the ensign's promise, a car was waiting to transport me to the base when the *Joy* pulled into port after one of its patrols. The driver of the navy car was a second lieutenant. A young captain sat in the passenger's seat up front.

I felt like I'd known the men all my life as we drove approximately ten miles to the base. I'd really been missing the warmth and unity of spirit that only Christians can share.

They informed me that tonight's OCF function was not a Bible study, but a dinner party for the OCF members and their wives.

When we arrived at the base, I could see lights streaming from the windows of the dining hall. Inside the building was a sizable gathering of men and women, and a long table filled with delicious-looking food.

"Just help yourself, Ross," the captain said. "You're our guest."

I immediately decided to forego the mingling for the time being and feast on the fine spread against the wall. As I sampled the chilled shrimp, finger sandwiches, and hors d'oeuvres, I realized how much I'd been missing while I was aboard ship.

The captain who accompanied me to the base walked up beside me while I was reaching for a particularly interesting-looking tidbit cut in the shape of a fish.

"Good stuff, huh?" he chuckled. "The officers' wives on base whipped up most of this."

"Yeah," I mumbled through my food. *If the OCF chapter here offers the same quality of spiritual food as it does physical food,* I thought, *I might just put in for an immediate transfer port side.*

The company proved to be as satisfying as the tasty fare. Everyone went out of their way to make me feel like a part of the group. I was disappointed when the first couples started to leave around 2200 hours (10:00 P.M.).

During the evening one young couple of newlyweds showed an unusual amount of interest in me. The young lieutenant, Carl Fetzer, was a muscular, attractive navy ex-aviator who had asked to be assigned ground duty after being married. His wife, Joan, was one of the most beautiful women I had ever seen. She was a petite brunette, with a flawless complexion and big, blue eyes that looked strangely sad.

I had to admit I was pretty impressed by them. But what on earth did they see in me that caused them to follow me around, laugh at all my jokes, and toward the end of the evening invite me to their home?

"Joan's promised me I could have an OCF party in our home," Carl laughed. "We hope you can be there."

I nodded politely. "I'll certainly do everything I can to be there. After this wingding tonight, I'd like to transfer on base permanently. You people know how to throw a party."

"This is our first OCF get-together ourselves," he informed me. "We've only been married for a couple of months. I was stationed here after getting my transfer from the aviation division."

"Well, we'll grow together in this fellowship," I said, noticing a rather peculiar, almost sour expression on Joan's face. "The Lord seems to be working in a lot of the officers' lives here."

Carl cleared his throat nervously. "Listen, Ross," he began, "how about coming over to our house here on the base tomorrow night?" He looked at his wife, who showed no expression at all. "We'll have some dinner, and . . ." He deliberated with his words. "And talk about . . . things."

"Yeah, fine," I said. "I'll have to clear it first with my shore patrol partners. But I'm sure they won't mind."

"Great," Carl said. "I'll meet you at the docks with a cab about 1830 hours."

The following evening at the appointed time, I exited the ship to find Carl standing beside the cab. He waved excitedly when he saw me coming.

"Hey, Ross," he said, shaking my hand. "Gee, I'm glad you could make it. Feel like some pot roast?"

"Yeah," I said, smacking my lips. "I welcome a meal away from our mess decks any time I can get one."

Riding in the cab to his home, Carl seemed slightly ill-at-ease. Finally, I got up the courage to ask if anything was wrong.

"No," he said, not very convincingly. "No. Well, not really."

"What is it?" I asked. "Am I imposing on you two? Is that it?"

"No, no," Carl said. "That's not it at all. Um, you see, I've only been a Christian for a few months. As a matter of fact, I became a believer just before Joan and I got married."

He thought momentarily. "The problem is Joan's not a Christian. Not only does she have no desire to be, but she thinks it's all a load of garbage. She gets angry every time I mention something about it."

"I can see where that would be a problem," I said. "I could sense she wasn't terribly thrilled with the company last night."

"You're right, she wasn't," he said. "But she seemed taken by you. She thought you were charming and funny, and you're about our age. So I hung around you last night hoping she'd loosen up some."

All of a sudden, I had the sinking feeling I was being used. But I also recognized a golden opportunity to share my faith and possibly enhance the marriage of a Christian brother.

"Do you want me to witness to her?" I asked. "You want me to say anything about the faith or not?"

"Not unless it just comes up naturally," he replied. "I've learned to steer clear of the subject unless she brings it up."

We rode in silence for the remainder of the cab ride. Finally we pulled up in front of his house. Carl paid for the taxi and we went in.

Joan was standing in the small living room of their home looking as lovely as ever. The aroma of home-cooked food filled the air.

"Smell's good," I said with a smile. "She's not only pretty," I said, turning to Carl, "she can cook."

Joan laughed appreciatively. "Well, you may change your mind after dinner," she said. "I've never cooked a pot roast before."

During an excellent dinner, the three of us talked about the ongoing Berlin Crisis and our individual duties. Carl looked like he couldn't be happier. Joan, however, looked undoubtedly less content. After finishing our meal, Carl suggested we go into the living room and sit down.

Joan appeared from the kitchen, wiping her hands on her apron, and stepped with obvious hesitation into the living room.

"Ross, would you like some coffee?" she asked.

"Yes, that would be nice."

She returned a short while later and poured three cups for each of us.

There was stiffness in her smile as she handed me the coffee.

"Uh, Ross tells me his wife and daughter are up to their necks in snow," Carl said, eager to break the uncomfortable silence.

"Yes, uh, they're really getting it, according to Pat," I said. "Almost a foot in several days. I hated having to leave them up there."

"How long have you been married?" Joan asked.

"About two years," I said. "Lord willing, our marriage won't be a total shambles by the time I get back."

I immediately regretted my words—on two counts.

Joan's face suddenly became stern. She leaned forward and looked intently at me.

"Ross, I'd like you to help us solve something, if you don't mind," she said.

"Uh, no," I said, taken a little off guard.

"It's about this upcoming party I agreed to host for some of Carl's buddies and their wives."

"Yes?"

"I had no idea it was a Christian group. He didn't say a word to me about that. Now he's asking me to sit in on some kind of Bible talk or something."

She gave Carl a reproving look. "I don't want this stuff crammed down my throat," she added. Carl grimaced. "I think you understand, don't you? I've got rights, too. The party doesn't have to include a discussion about religion, does it? You don't go in for all that Bible stuff, do you?"

Talk about being on the hot seat! I felt the steam rising through my collar. If I answered no, I'd be lying and Carl would probably never forgive me. If I answered yes, I knew she'd feel as if she'd been set up tonight. A yes answer was going to stir up a hornet's nest, I knew, but I couldn't back down.

"Yes, I do happen to believe the Bible and what it says about salvation through Christ," I said.

"Oh, great," she said indignantly, barely letting me finish my sentence. "Another Holy Roller. The place is crawlin' with 'em."

"Calm down, Joan," Carl interjected sharply. "Let him finish what he was going to say."

"So he can save my soul, right?" she shot back. "You wanted to bring him here for that. Admit it, Carl."

"Joan, I don't have the power to save you. Only God can do that. He does love you," I said.

She stood up angrily and removed her apron. "Why do you people act so condescending, like I'm the world's biggest sinner," she remarked coldly. "Everywhere I go someone's always trying to put me down."

She walked toward the kitchen and turned back.

"I don't know what these people have been feeding you, Carl," she said. "But it's about to ruin our marriage."

I inched forward in my chair. "Joan, putting your faith in Christ is the best thing a couple can do for their marriage. It can strengthen a marriage. I know mine is better because of the faith my wife and I have."

She stood with her arms folded and a smirk on her face. I sensed she was only giving me enough rope so she could hang me with it.

"I wish you'd read Billy Graham's book, *Peace with God,*" I said. "I've got a copy of it on the ship. I'd love for you to have it. You'll see that Christ came and died so we could really live." I shook my head. "It's not something to be ashamed of. It's a gift. A great gift."

"Get yourself out of this house!" Her words rose in intensity as she spat them out. "I never want to see you again. Don't come around here." She wheeled in the direction of Carl, who was standing horrified across the room.

"And you can forget that party, Carl. I won't have any part of it." She seemed on the verge of tears. "And you can forget our marriage, too."

With that she spun away, walked down the hall, and slammed her bedroom door.

"Carl, I gotta get out of here," I said in a trembling voice. My face felt drained of color. "I'm sorry."

He caught me before I walked out the door. "Ross, gosh, I'm the one that's sorry. I don't know what's wrong with her. Listen, I'll call you a cab, OK?"

"Fine, Carl. I'll wait for it outside."

I walked out into the night, utterly shocked at what had just taken place. My knees were so weak I could barely stand. The strain of my shipboard duties seemed tame compared to the lions' den I'd just escaped.

Even the Cubans respond better to my witness than that, I thought.

Perhaps I was feeling too big for my spiritual britches, but I had sincerely expected to lead her to Christ and see their marriage take on a new proportion.

I sighed in relief when the cab finally showed up. I'd been petrified that Joan would come out the front door any minute and start on me again.

After getting back to the ship, I went directly to the

forecastle, where I sometimes led church services on Sundays and spent time in prayer and meditation. I sat down in one of the folding metal chairs and cradled my head in my hands.

I've learned my lesson, I said to myself. *All my zeal and witnessing have caused more harm than good.*

I turn people away from me; I make them laugh at me; and now I've ruined a marriage. That's it. If God wants a witness, it'll have to be somebody else. I'm through.

I thought my attitude would change after several days, but it didn't. No longer did I share with anyone what God had done for me. Struggling with guilt for having virtually abandoned my family, I couldn't think of anything he had done lately, anyway.

As ship's chaplain, my sermons on Sundays began to lack the punch and verve with which I'd delivered them in the past. And while I still kept up my periods of meditation—reading the Bible, memorizing Scripture, and trying to apply it to my life—I didn't read and pray as I had before; I didn't ask God to teach me so I could teach others. I was too confused about my own spirituality to help anyone else.

Only twenty minutes on the wrong end of a harangue by an irate, non-Christian woman had dried up my spiritual fountain—maybe for good.

I saw Carl several times at subsequent OCF meetings during the rest of my brief time in Guantánamo Bay, but the subject of his wife was never raised. I got the impression from him that he was attending the Bible studies without her knowledge. He did say once that he had purchased a copy of the Graham book *Peace with God* and left it where Joan could pick it up and read it if she desired.

Four years later, while I was struggling to get through my junior year of medical school at the University of Florida,

I pulled an *OCF Newsletter* from the usual bundle of bills in the day's mail.

Thumbing through it before going to bed, I was nearly knocked out of my chair with surprise. There, in a black-and-white photograph, were Carl and Joan Fetzer. The headline above the accompanying story read: "Fetzers: Committed Couple for Christ."

"Whoa!" I said in disbelief. I fell back, openmouthed, and devoured every word in the article written by the attractive couple. It was a testimony of how Christ had entered their lives and brought harmony out of conflict while Carl was stationed in Guantánamo Bay, Cuba, through the witness of one Lieutenant Ross Campbell.

I didn't try to hold back the tears. I wept as I read that it had been the book *Peace with God* by Billy Graham, which I had recommended, that had enabled the couple to avert divorce. Both of them had read it and become a wonderfully dynamic team in the kingdom of God.

Although I had recovered my spiritual balance a few weeks after the incident in the Fetzer's home, I was now waging another spiritual battle due to the mental retardation of my second daughter. The exciting news about the Fetzers was like a soothing spiritual balm.

Pat was also deeply moved when I showed her the article. It said the couple was currently stationed in Jacksonville, roughly one hundred and fifty miles from our home in Gainesville.

"Why don't we invite them over here?" Pat suggested.

I wrinkled my brow in thought. The idea of seeing the couple again after all these years was exciting—and a little scary. I felt a twinge of anxiety surface in me as I thought back to the unpleasant encounter I'd had with Joan at their home. But, according to this article, Joan was "a new creature." I was anxious to see what the Lord had wrought in her life.

"Well, OK," I said. "It'd be interesting. What a difference four years appear to have made."

After several calls to the base in Jacksonville, I finally

located Carl. He was ecstatic to hear my voice.

"Ross! Man, it's great to hear from you," he exclaimed. "We think about you often. How'd you know we were here?"

"From the article in the OCF paper," I replied. "What a great feature."

Carl was thrilled we had seen the article and immediately began making plans over the phone for the two of them to travel to Gainesville. Several weekends later the couple appeared on our front doorstep, beaming from ear to ear. The Lord had accomplished more in their lives than even I had anticipated. Joan, who was as lovely as ever, had indeed become a new person. In her blue eyes, where I had once detected a deep sadness, was a dancing radiance.

What a shot in the arm. The charge that went through me as a result of seeing the two of them and their printed testimony remained with me for a long, long time. I was moved by God's amazing power to transform lives in unforeseen ways through deeds and words that seemed at the time to be wholly insignificant, even counterproductive.

▶*Cast thy bread upon the waters: for thou shalt find it after many days* (Eccles. 11:1, KJV).

▶*God's ways are behind the scenes, but He moves all the scenes which He is behind* (John Nelson Darby).

CHAPTER

"WHERE ARE YOU, GOD?"

I stood motionless in the doorway of the bedroom, gripped by the horrible, helpless sight that had become miserably commonplace for our family. I ran my hand through my hair in distress, and let my arm drop limply as I struggled to control the thoughts slamming together inside my head. Our three-year-old daughter Cathy lay on her bed experiencing a seizure for the second time in two days.

The knot in my stomach tightened with each moment our little girl remained locked in the fixed, painfully listless state symptomatic of her cerebral palsy. Looking at Pat, I could see she, too, was troubled. Yet somehow she stayed calm before the same agonizing scene that in me produced waves of rage, guilt, and even physical pain in my stomach.

"I can't bear to see her like this anymore," I groaned.

"It's just too hard to see her getting worse and worse."

Tears had begun to well up in Pat's eyes. She bit her upper lip and silently nodded her head. "I know," she uttered softly.

Overcome by emotion, I stomped to the back of our small Gainesville, Florida, house and burst out the back door, slamming it behind me. I aimlessly walked out into the night, stopping to lean against the rusted clothesline post in our tiny backyard and look up into the starlit sky. I was tempted to keep walking, to simply run away and shed this torturous predicament for good. But that notion evaporated as quickly as it had come: I was bound to this nightmare. Running away would not free me of the burdens that threatened to crush my family.

Being in my junior year of medical school with two children was taxing enough emotionally and financially. But with Cathy's palsy-related seizure disorder worsening, our lives were literally crumbling before our eyes.

Carey, our first child, had been born—as nearly as we could tell—perfect. Cathy, our second, had been born with a club foot. Initially, we believed this deformity, which was devastating enough for us, was the extent of her disability. At about a year old, however, during the time I was finishing up my career in the navy, Cathy began to experience brief periods of blanking out, for want of a better description; her eyes would become fixed in a terrified stare and her little body would suddenly freeze in place.

These seizures usually lasted no more than several seconds. When Cathy would come to, a frightened, confused look would cross her face and she'd begin crying. In several months' time, the seizures became accompanied by telltale tremors in her hands, which intensified gradually until there was little doubt something was seriously wrong with our baby daughter. Only time would tell, we were told repeatedly, the extent to which Cathy was incapacitated.

At eighteen months Cathy had still failed to perform the normal tasks for a child her age—sitting, standing, and saying simple words. During Cathy's first year and a half of life, our friends made feeble efforts to reassure us that Cathy would be fine. We hoped she would somehow turn out normal and make up for lost time—a common hope among parents of retarded children.

As the months passed, the hopes faded and the harsh realities set in. It was only a short time later, just following my entrance into medical school at the University of Florida, that our fears were confirmed. The diagnosis came after a battery of tests at the university medical center.

The doctor's announcement that Cathy had a neurological disorder, later diagnosed as ataxic cerebral palsy, cut into me like a jagged knife. Shortly thereafter we learned there was a better than 60 percent chance that severe mental retardation would result from Cathy's cerebral palsy.

My gnawing anxiety naturally hindered my ability to concentrate on my studies. My first year of medical school became the most miserable year of my life. A dream to become a medical missionary had developed during my navy days when I had seen the suffering in so many lands. Now my dream seemed doomed, but I continued on with my schooling, despite nearly flunking out in that critical first year.

Pat and I desperately sought a means to improve Cathy's condition with no success, until someone suggested we employ patterning methods (more specifically, the Doman and Delacato patterning method researched and recommended by the Philadelphia Neurological Institute), which had recently come into vogue.

We were informed by a local pediatrician, whom I held in great respect, that this new technique was bringing about amazing results. Retarded children were actually being cured, we were told, by the technique, which called for parents and other adults to assist the retarded child in simulated crawling.

The basic premise behind patterning is that a young child's mind develops based upon his ability to perform certain physical functions, such as rolling and crawling. Proponents of the technique insisted—and still do— that since retarded children bypass the crawling stage, which is crucial in the early development of children, patterning is a logical method for aiding the development of a retarded child. By exercising specific motor patterns for Cathy, we were led to believe that we could retrain or recircuit her damaged central nervous system.

With some skepticism, I questioned the benefits of the practice, believing that retarded children lack the neurophysiological faculties to respond to the behavior being thrust upon them. However, the pediatrician was so urgent in outlining the method of treatment for Cathy that we were finally persuaded to begin the exercises.

We quickly discovered how involved and physically and mentally draining the method is: It requires five adults—one at each limb and one at the head—to manipulate the child to mimic the crawling movement during daily five-hour sessions.

I'll never forget the blank, worn expressions on the faces of Pat and some of our friends as we methodically worked Cathy's little body in unison. The sessions became an absurd, almost surreal drudgery that we continued for many months. We were afraid to stop because of the inevitable guilt we'd feel in doing so.

When our whole lives began to revolve around these grueling patterning sessions, naturally, our family suffered. Carey, who was five at the time, had it as tough as anyone. Her irritable, whining demands had a poor effect on our already frayed nerves. And little else but angry talk began filling the time I spent with Pat.

We simply no longer operated as a family. Much of our time and energy was spent pursuing this technique. Worst of all, the tedious hours we spent working Cathy's limbs and head bore no results whatsoever. In fact, our daughter's condition deteriorated.

At the end of nearly six months of the prescribed patterning regimen, with no rewards to show for our diligence, I felt as if I'd been duped.

Many practitioners and parents alike have since come forth discrediting the Doman-Delacato patterning method. These statements of disavowal only reinforce the conclusion I reached after our experience with Cathy that the patterning technique was developed without scientific basis and its premise is espoused on totally shaky grounds.

Cathy was nearing her fourth birthday as we returned hopelessly to square one in her treatment. On her birthday there would be cake and presents, but none of the usual happiness that traditionally surrounds the anniversary of a child's birth—only the devastating knowledge that she was oblivious to the fun of childhood and that her profound retardation was becoming more manifest daily.

At first, there had been the prolonged periods when Cathy would refuse to eat; then, the observable seizures commenced, growing more pronounced and frequent in her second and third years until they were coming at a rate of two to three a month.

Cathy had become so sensitive by this time that the slightest interruption in her environment would bring on a seizure. Merely taking her from the outdoors into the house, or vice versa, or removing her from the sunshine or the shade would plunge her system into chaos.

Doctors introduced one anti-seizure drug and then another to combat Cathy's worsening disorder, all of which proved ineffective and left serious side effects. Dosages were increased, but the situation steadily worsened. We watched helplessly as the grip of the affliction that had seized our daughter grew more powerful and resistant to our efforts.

The seizures left Cathy so physically spent and groggy that she was unable to eat for a period of about three days. Her body weight plummeted to that of a child half her age. When the seizures began happening every other day, overlapping into the three-day recovery periods, severe malnutrition and dehydration began to threaten her life. Forced tube feeding in the hospital was the only way to keep her alive following a convulsion.

Making matters worse was Cathy's physiological craving for stimulation. Her inadequate sense of touch forced her to extreme behavior in order to get any kind of sensation. To our horror, Cathy would continually try to place her hands on the burners of the stove while it was in use. And her voracious appetite, attributable mostly to the prolonged periods she went without food following a seizure, sent her digging in the garbage to satisfy herself between meals.

We were perpetually confronted with our inability to safely care for our daughter. A change called out to be made, but each option open to us offered heartache of a different kind.

I draped my wrists over the T-shaped clothesline post for support, muttering repeatedly the only word that would surface in my jumbled thoughts: Why?

Why? Why is this happening? How on earth can we survive? I wanted to scream, but I stifled the urge for the sake of the neighbors who shared our crowded little block of housing near the university campus.

Cathy's medical bills had thrown our meager budget into a vicious spin months ago. We had already made three trips to the hospital in two months to prevent Cathy from becoming dehydrated.

This next trip will finally break us, I thought.

A generous $6,000 inheritance received from a late uncle just after my stint in the navy had been earmarked for my medical training. Now that money, too, was perilously close to being exhausted due to repeated withdrawals. Already three months late in paying our electricity bill, with delinquency notices piling up on the desk, we lived daily with the fear that our family could be plunged at any minute into a darkness more tangible than any we might be experiencing inwardly.

The prospect of having to proceed with additional treatment for Cathy expanded our bleak situation to tragic proportions. Furthermore, it was becoming more and more apparent that we were on the verge of either hiring a full-time nurse to care for Cathy or losing our three-year-old to an institution. Either development could serve the final blow that would send us into bankruptcy.

Unlike much of my time in the navy, I had my family around me, yet I could not remember ever feeling more vulnerable or alone. I had made it to this point in medical school on sheer guts and determination. But, now, having come so far, it appeared my resolve and money had at last worn thin.

Now Cathy's seizures had developed into severe jerking movements. Struggling to purge the devastating sight of her uncontrollable movements from my memory, I tried to pray. But my attempts were futile. I was just too numb to assemble my fears and shattered hopes and communicate them to God. I doubted he was offering the miracles I needed, anyway.

Cathy has steadily gotten worse since she was born, I told myself bitterly. *Why should I expect God to intervene now?*

Wallowing in self-pity, my long pent-up feelings of frustration turned to anger and bitter defiance. My future had seemed so promising. After my term in the navy, I had thought, I would get my medical degree and set off with my family to the mission field happily to serve God as best I knew how. But it hadn't taken long before all of my best laid plans fell apart.

Now I was the father of a severely handicapped child and the head of a severely troubled household.

"God, deliver me," I muttered softly. "Give me just one break. I've been faithful. Why have you forsaken me? Why have you forsaken me when I need you most?"

I realized how closely my statements resembled those of Christ on the cross. *Christ's suffering had a purpose,* I thought. *If there's a purpose in mine, Lord, I wish I could see it.*

God's comfort gradually soothed me. I knew he would not leave us alone.

I felt Pat's hand on my shoulder.

"It's over," she said quietly. "She's resting now. Come on inside and I'll fix you some dinner before we leave for the hospital."

Pat called the hospital to alert them of our coming, then phoned a friend to come over and sit with Carey. There was no rush in getting Cathy there, now that the convulsion was over and she was resting; the tube feeding would actually not be necessary for another eight hours or so. If things remained true to form, she'd remain in this post-seizure, semi-paralyzed state for three days.

I flopped down in my chair at the dinner table and listened as Pat began the debate on what our next step should be. As I expected, she immediately suggested she return to teaching to pick up some extra money. She'd managed to complete her degree by sheer determination, but had quit her work several years ago because of the fearful reaction of our daughter Carey, who was then four, to her mother's absences. I had only recently rejected another offer by Pat to return to work, but with things growing steadily more grave, I heard her argument with a different mind.

Another option, which hurt to think about, was for me

to quit medical school and take a job. To do so meant throwing away nearly a whole semester of work and two previous years of intense effort and hard-earned savings already spent in the University of Florida's medical program.

"Carey is older now," Pat pointed out. "I think she would get along much better. We don't really have much of a choice. We're nearly down to our last fifty dollars, and we've got to pay that electricity bill."

As Pat talked, I noticed how faded and frayed her dress looked. Though she sorely needed new clothing, she had not bought a new dress in months. This only added to my guilt. I sighed deeply and cradled my head in my hands. *How did we ever get in this mess?* I thought.

"OK, Pat. See if you can find part-time work first. I can't bear to see Carey suffer from all of this, too."

"I'll start looking right away," she said. "We'll pray about it, Ross," she said confidently, patting my hand. "God doesn't always meet our wants, but he'll meet our needs. He keeps his eye on the sparrows."

"If we were sparrows, we'd be in a lot better shape," I said, joking. "There'd certainly be less heartache."

Carey entered the room. The long-mouthed expression on her little face demonstrated how much she was being affected by Cathy's unpredictable condition.

"Can I give Cathy some of my food?" our six-year-old asked. "I don't want her to be sick."

"That's OK, honey," Pat said. "We're going to make sure Cathy gets something to eat. Don't worry."

I placed my hand on top of my little girl's head and looked at her lovingly through the building tears. That was just like Carey. She was the most caring and sensitive child I had ever seen. Her feelings were so fragile. The hurt she was obviously experiencing multiplied the anguish I already felt.

"I love you, Carey," I said. "You're a good girl. Everything's going to be OK."

I cringed initially at making such a glib promise, but

as I surveyed the delicate, trusting face of our eldest daughter, the ache in my heart suddenly began to disappear. The protective love I felt for Carey caused my resolve to reemerge. A surge of inner peace and warmth swept through me as I felt God move among us. Shrugging off my self-pity and the awareness of my own human fragility, I vowed to myself, *With God's help, I'll make everything OK.*

" 'I can do all things through Christ who strengthens me,' " I said to Carey. "Have you ever heard that verse before?" She shook her head no. "Well, it's a good one. We need to remember it."

It was nearly 8:30 in the evening. The sun's drop from the sky had little or no effect on the stifling temperature inside our unair-conditioned dwelling. I hadn't been very hungry, and I stared down on my plate of half-eaten food. As I moved my food around the plate with my fork and tried to come up with ideas for getting extra money. I knew Cathy's coming stay in the hospital would wipe out all of our money, including the account we used for funding my education.

It's in your hands, Lord, I prayed silently at the table. *You'll have to show us the way.*

We were sitting in the living room, with Cathy bundled in a thin blanket, when the sitter arrived.

Carey ran up to us as we stood to leave. "I don't want you to go," she whimpered. Her face suddenly became serious as she turned to the sitter. "But Cathy's sick. She needs to go to the hospital, doesn't she, Mama?"

"That's right, honey," Pat said. "We'll be back soon."

"We're praying for all of you," the sitter said. "This must be an awfully hard time for your family."

"Thanks."

"I'm praying, too," Carey chipped in.

Pat knelt to hug Carey. "You keep praying," she said, wiping the moisture from her eyes with a free hand. "God hears every one of your prayers."

I carried Cathy outside in my arms and handed her over to Pat on the passenger's side. A flash of lightning illuminated a bank of storm clouds moving in our direction. I shrugged off the idea of going back in the house to get an umbrella.

"We can use the rain," Pat said. "The heat has been unbearable lately."

Fortunately, we were only five minutes from the university hospital, because the needle in the gas gauge was resting just above the empty mark. Heading down our street, we noticed the wind had picked up considerably.

Intermittent rain splattered on the windshield as we rounded the corner onto the street where the university medical complexes are located. Wind gusts whistled through the loose-fitting cracks of our car windows and swayed the huge palms lining the sidewalks. We traveled in silence, watching the tall palms rocking from side to side. I jumped suddenly in my seat, gasping, as a frond was ripped from the crest of one of the trees and slapped against the hood of our car. My action showed us both just how edgy I was.

As the storm whipped the palm trees above us, I saw in them a parallel with my own life.

The trees bend, but they don't break, I thought, *because their roots are strong. Is this why I haven't broken . . . although I feel as if I'm ready to?*

I knew my Christian roots could be stronger, but I hated to think of the state we'd be in if it weren't for our faith in God's goodness and just purposes. Despite our convictions, we were not immune to doubts. This prevailing family crisis had taken a toll on our spiritual perspective.

Though at times we had been tempted to deny that God truly cared or to believe that we were being punished, we still felt that God hurt as much, if not more, than either of us over Cathy's condition. With his strength, we were able to refuse to make our trust in his power and love contingent on whether or not he intervened in Cathy's situation.

We struggled daily with the issue of God's will in this matter, but we tried not to expect answers to all of our questions. As it had occurred to me in the backyard just hours before, Christ had questioned God, especially at the height of his agony on the cross, but he submitted to God's will nonetheless. And in his pain and death, there unquestionably had been a great victory.

What a hard lesson for mortals to learn, I reflected.

I recalled a little saying I'd seen on a small plaque in a friend's house: "Sometimes the Lord calms the storm; sometimes He lets the storm rage and calms His child."

What an appropriate commentary on my situation. I prayed the Lord would calm me, because it was obvious he was allowing the storm in my life to rage.

As we approached the university medical center, I caught sight of the wing where Cathy had been diagnosed as having cerebral palsy. The thought of that room, with its cold, white tile and stainless steel tables, conjured up painful memories. Cathy's dehumanizing testing at the hands of an abrupt, insensitive doctor marked the beginning, for me at least, of a building emotional crisis I would deal with fully only years later.

The trauma of the experience came rushing back. I recalled the cold nature of the head doctor—a disastrous quality, I had thought, for a practitioner assigned to deal with distraught parents looking for answers regarding their children.

The room had seemed filled with the entire hospital staff, including the residents, interns, and medical students. Upon our entrance, the doctor had ordered Pat to remove all of Cathy's clothing and place her in the middle of the floor at their feet. Pat did as she was told, and slowly lowered Cathy to the hard linoleum floor.

For several moments, Cathy had just lain there essentially doing nothing. Finally, she got on her hands and knees and made a poor, awkward attempt at crawling. It was a grotesque sight for me to watch my little daughter, without clothes, wriggling uncoordinatedly across the floor while all of these people stroked their chins and whispered opinions among themselves.

"There's something wrong with her brain," the head doctor announced in a gruff, unemotional tone.

After briefly conferring with his colleagues, he left the room. And that was it—no efforts at consoling us, no recommendations for Cathy's further care, no comparisons with other cases, nothing.

At first I was dumbfounded by the doctor's crass attitude. Then I became angry. I wanted to give the doctor a piece of my mind for his smugness and uncaring attitude, but I held my tongue.

A member of the evaluation team had informed Pat that she could dress Cathy. Neither of us had spoken, but I was certain everyone in the room was receiving a message loud and clear from the perturbed expression on my face.

"I'm sorry," the attendant said finally. "We'll get you a test report just as soon as we can. There'll be some recommendations in it for handling your daughter's treatment."

Later, owing mostly to my disgruntlement over the head doctor's harsh method, I wrote off the test report drawn up by the staff. I couldn't bear to see the label of mentally retarded placed on Cathy; it served as the final punctuation to a miserable, eighteen-month-long series of events.

"They're wrong," I'd insisted to Pat. "This isn't possible." But with the passage of time, the findings proved accurate.

Now, a torturous year and a half later, I pulled up to the entrance of the medical center's emergency room. After dropping off Pat and Cathy, I parked the car and rejoined Pat in the lobby; Cathy had already been taken to the children's intensive care ward. I slumped into one of the emergency room chairs to wait while Pat filled out the necessary paperwork.

Just about the time she completed the forms, a friend who was serving his residency at the medical center entered the room.

"I'm awfully sorry about your daughter's condition," he said. "I saw her coming in. I'm on duty tonight, so I'll see she's well taken care of."

"Thanks very much."

"This must be a terrific strain on you two."

"Boy, you've said it," I replied. "It looks as if Pat's going back to work teaching. That's the only way we can see to pay our bills and keep me in school."

My friend thought a minute, fumbling with the stethoscope around his neck. "You know, there's a school in town here that cares for severely retarded children," he said. "I think it's a free service that operates three or four days a week. You might look into it if it's necessary for you to work, Pat."

We hadn't heard of the school, but we had certainly been made harshly familiar with several so-called free service agencies for retarded children in Gainesville. Unbelievably, a bias seemed to exist against medical students at these agencies, making it nearly impossible for us to obtain use of appliances, corrective shoes, braces, and other special equipment for Cathy. I told my friend that had such help been available to us, we might not have a stack of delinquent power bills on our desk.

"I'm not about to go and beg from these people," I said.

"Oh, I don't think you'll have to," he replied.

He paused, deliberating slightly before he spoke.

"Have you all considered placing Cathy in an institution where she can receive around-the-clock care?" he asked delicately.

Pat sighed heavily. "Yes, we have. I don't see how we really can carry on like we're doing without some help. Taking Cathy anywhere, creating any interruption in her environment, brings on a seizure."

"Yeah, I'm aware of that," he said solemnly. "When she was exposed to the bright lights of the children's ward, she went into another seizure. We made her as comfortable as we could." He paused to read our reaction, then continued. "I don't see how you can go on without any help," he said.

"Well, we can't go on without any help," I reiterated, realizing how rich in meaning my statement was. "We need miracles from heaven."

"Well," he chuckled softly, "I don't know where you can pick up any miracles, but the Gainesville school might be willing to look at your case. And," he paused to think, "there are some excellent state-operated institutions for retarded children that are supposed to be very good for permanent care. Sunland, I think they're called. The closest to us, I believe, is in Tallahassee."

I thanked my friend for his concern and his help. By 10:30 we were in our car heading home. Pat looked very tired, but somehow relieved. I guessed the information we'd received had eased her mind somewhat; plus, we'd made the decision that she could begin working again.

Teaching was definitely her calling—and the diversion from her problems would do her good, I concluded. She was so good with children. *What a shame,* I thought before rolling over to sleep that night, *that Cathy should have such a fine mother and yet not know it.*

In several months' time, Cathy was enrolled for day care in the Sunshine School in Gainesville, and Pat, after a brief time of searching, nailed down a substitute teaching position. Now we could begin making payments on the bills piled up by Cathy's hospitalization.

➡️*Blessed be the LORD, because he hath heard the voice of my supplications* (Ps. 28:6, KJV).
➡️*Sometimes the Lord calms the storm; sometimes He lets the storm rage and calms His child* (Author unknown).

CHAPTER

DESPERATION AND DELIVERANCE

When I entered my junior year at the University of
Florida Medical School in 1966, it was a time of national
upheaval. Storm clouds of protest and disenchantment
were overtaking the once calm landscape of a stable
America. American soldiers were just beginning to fight
in Southeast Asia, and inflation posed a growing threat
to the nation's economy. But in our own home, the
ramifications of a torn society were of little consequence
as we faced a more consuming, personal battle.

For a while it looked as if some degree of normalcy in
our lives was possible. Then, as a result of Pat's extended
periods away from home, Carcy's usual sweetness turned
sour.

Pat's absenses from home produced intense anxiety in
our oldest daughter, throwing her delicate, once secure
world into a whirl. Our only option was for Pat to quit

teaching. Once again we were back at square one in the vicious game of meeting our day-to-day financial needs.

Each day brought us closer to the brink of bankruptcy, as Cathy's medical bills grew to astronomical proportions. Finally, the day arrived when our finances were completely exhausted.

I decided I'd drop in on Pat between my classes and have lunch, thinking the surprise would brighten her day. She was surprised all right: I found her crying softly at the desk in our living room. Her hand rested on a stack of unpaid bills.

Her reddened eyes were already focused on me as I entered the room.

"Ross, we have got to do something to get money," she sobbed. "Our electricity bill is so far past due. This notice"—she waved a piece of paper in her hand—"says if the bill is not paid by Monday, they're going to cut off our power."

I walked quickly to her and embraced her where she sat. "Oh, Pat. Please don't cry. I'll think of something."

She laid down the notice and stood up. "I've already decided. I'm going to ask my folks for enough money to pay our power bill and Cathy's hospital bills for the month," she said between sniffs.

"And . . . I'm going to look for a job again," she added.

I collapsed angrily in a chair. "There's no way you can work. Carey can't tolerate it, you know that. She becomes petrified when you leave. And you're not going to call anyone. Our parents don't have the money to give anymore. They've helped us beyond their means already."

I leaned forward and tried to look reassuring. "I told you to give me a chance to think of something."

Pat remained silent, having said her piece. She was waiting for this brainstorm I kept telling her I was about to have.

At the time, G.I. benefits had been frozen, to our utter

chagrin. We'd hoped they would gear back up before we depleted the $6,000 inheritance received from my uncle for medical school, but they hadn't. I knew we'd reached a dead end, but I thought I had one final option.

"I'll go to the office of student affairs and see if I can't find a part-time night job on campus," I said. "That'll give us enough money to get over the hump."

Pat shook her head slowly. "But what about right now, Ross? You can't get a paycheck in four days, even if you get a job today."

"I'll ask for an advance."

Pat glared at me, as if to say, "Come on." She was right. Who was I kidding? We both knew I was making empty promises.

"I'm going to call my folks," she said.

"No, Pat. At least give me until Friday, all right?"

She hesitated for a moment. "OK. Friday."

I ate quickly and headed for the front door. I was already going to be late for my 1:40 lecture. Pat looked up from the desk as I opened the door to leave.

"Pat, please don't worry," I said. "I promise I'll think of something. Something will happen. It'll be OK."

She smiled faintly. "I hope so."

Stepping out into the bright afternoon sunshine, I began thinking of the possibilities open to me for getting my family through this life-threatening period. Quitting school was out of the question; that was the one thing I was certain of. I'd come too far to quit.

I still didn't have any other solution as I reached the campus outskirts but to find a part-time job. *It's gonna kill me. This semester's already hard enough,* I thought.

As I walked I prayerfully outlined my situation. A strong sensation of God's presence overcame me. I realized I had no alternative other than to fully commit my burdens to him. I didn't view God as a kind of Divine Troubleshooter; but I knew he'd never allowed me to suffer more than I could bear. Somehow I'd managed to come out of every scrape OK, even when the very worst looked bound to happen.

I'll let go, then.

Feeling God's hand on my shoulder, I turned to my studies.

At the end of my last afternoon class, I headed to the library to complete some research I needed to do for a paper. While buried in my work, I suddenly remembered my lunchtime conversation with Pat.

"Oh, no," I said aloud. The clock on the library wall showed 4:55. Quickly, I gathered my books and dashed toward the student center and the office of student affairs. The door was locked when I arrived.

"Blast it!" I muttered. "Now what do I do?"

I shuffled away, feeling angry and guilty that I'd been so negligent in following through with the promise I'd made to Pat. *I'll do it tomorrow,* I tried to console myself.

The presence of God I'd felt so often before was gone. I chided myself for having let my mood of resignation get the best of me. I looked for an excuse to cover my forgetfulness. *I'm just tired, I guess.*

Before walking home, I decided to check some test grades posted on the bulletin board in the chemistry building.

My mood was as bleak and hollow as the unlit, deserted hallway inside the two-story building. Only the reverberating clicks of my heels sounded in the empty corridor as I made my way to its far end.

With each step, the realization of how desperate our situation had become fell heavier upon me. I ignored my earlier confidence.

Lord, please, I pleaded. *I don't know how I'm going to deal with this. I can't solve these financial problems alone. There's no one to turn to but you.*

As I neared the bulletin board, I suddenly became

aware of another pair of shoes clicking further down the
hallway. I stopped at the board to find my grades. The
steps grew louder and louder, until they suddenly ceased
directly behind me.

"Ross?" someone called out. "Is that you?"

I wheeled quickly and saw a smiling, youthful,
familiar-looking face. I studied him for an instant until I
was sure who it was. It was Frank Myers, an old navy
buddy who'd been stationed on the USS *Princeton* with
me in Long Beach, California. I hadn't seen him in years.

"Frank? Hey, how are ya?"

"Great, old buddy. What are you doing here in these
halls of higher learning?"

"Trying to get through medical school," I replied.
"How about yourself?"

He shrugged and smiled proudly. "You may not believe
this, but I've been asked by the university to begin a
new graduate program in the area of rehabilitation
counseling. It's the first such program in the country. I'm
working now to enlist students in the program." His eyes
suddenly lit up.

"Hey, Ross. You wouldn't be interested would you?
You'd make a great candidate."

"Who, me? No, no. I've got my hands full just trying
to finish medical school. I hope we don't starve before I
graduate."

"You don't understand, Ross. The program pays two
hundred dollars a month, and you only have to go to
school three to four hours a day. Can you believe that?"

"Boy, I could really use the two hundred dollars," I
said. "That would really help us. But I couldn't swing it.
Sorry. I've got all the academic load I can carry now."

"Well, OK," he said. "If you should run into anyone
who would fit the bill, tell them to give me a call." He
hurriedly wrote his name and number down on a scrap
of paper in his notebook and shoved it at me.

"Well, listen, Ross," he said. "I gotta run. But call me,

OK? We'll get together and talk about the old navy days."

"Yeah, Frank. I sure will."

I turned back around to the jumble of paper tacked on the board. My friend was nearly at the end of the hall and out the door when it hit me. *Pat. Pat could enroll in the program.*

"Hey, Frank," I hollered. "Wait up."

Pat was thrilled with the idea when I arrived home with the particulars on the program. She agreed that the opportunity to make an additional two hundred dollars a month while working toward a master's degree was too good to pass up.

But there was little celebration. The prospect of receiving two hundred dollars a month from the program, providing Pat was accepted, was great, but it did nothing to alleviate the debts that presently hung over us.

It was Wednesday. If nothing changed by the end of the week, I'd be studying by candlelight and we'd be taking cold showers, not to mention eating food out of a can.

"I'm calling home tomorrow," Pat said over dinner. "That's all. Unless you want to apply for a grant or take out a loan."

"Yeah," I moaned. "Fat chance of that with no credit."

I put down my fork and looked intently at Pat. "You can't keep asking our parents to bail us out!"

"Then we'd better start praying," Pat said. She laughed sourly. "Pray first of all that the power company loses our file."

The following day I decided to show up at home again for lunch. This time I'd made inquiries at the student affairs office about part-time work. They would let me know if some work became available. I emptied the mailbox on my way inside.

"Junk mail and . . ." I stopped as Pat entered the living room.

"Say it, Ross," she said. "More bills. Bills we can't pay."

I frowned and continued flipping through the stack. On one letter I recognized the handwriting of my grandfather.

"Huh, a letter from my grandfather," I said. "I hope everyone's OK. I haven't heard from him since I was in the navy."

Pat had finished preparing lunch and was seated at the desk, where she was completing the application to the master's program. She jumped at least a foot when I shouted.

"Look at this!" I hollered at the top of my lungs. "Look at this!"

"Shhh, Ross, you'll wake up Carey," Pat said. "What on earth is it?"

"Only a check," I said, gleefully waving the piece of paper in my hand. "A check for a thousand dollars!"

"What!" Pat screamed in astonishment. "Let me see."

"Yeah, look. I can't believe this. Why in the world would he send us a thousand dollars?"

Pat studied the check in disbelief. "God bless him," she said. Tears began to well up in her eyes. I hugged her in a long embrace. We both stood in the middle of the floor, crying and laughing together.

"What's going on?" Carey asked from the hallway. Our jubilation had awakened her from her afternoon nap. She walked into the living room rubbing her eyes.

"Honey, your Great-Granddad Campbell has sent us a lot of money. . . ." Pat looked up at me and smiled. "For what reason, I don't know."

"It's miraculous," I said. "It's an answer to prayer. There's no other explanation for it. You know my family hates to write. I can't imagine anyone telling Granddad we needed this money."

I pulled the folded paper out of the envelope and flipped it open. I read the brief message aloud: "Ross and Pat, I thought you all could use this. Hope things are improving for you. Good luck. Give my love to the kids. Love, Granddad."

"It is an answer to prayer," Pat said.

She jumped up quickly and wiped her eyes with her hands. "You know what I'm going to do?"

"What?" I smiled.

She reached out her hand for the check. "I'm going to the bank. And then I'm going to go pay a power bill."

"Aww, let's wait till Tuesday," I joked. "I'd like to have dinner by candlelight."

She laughed. "You have my permission to light every candle in the house."

God's guiding light had appeared again when our path was darkest. But though our home had been spared literal darkness, there was still a dark corner in the house—Cathy's bedroom—and a corresponding darkness in our hearts, as well.

With each passing day, the pressing decisions regarding Cathy's future hovered more ominously over our heads. Finally, her deteriorating physical condition shoved us to the brink of the inevitable, bitter reality we'd tried to avoid: The day school was not enough. Cathy had to be institutionalized. Without daily tube feeding and continuous hospital care, she would literally starve to death.

We began the one-hundred-and-fifty-mile trip north to Sunland in Tallahassee before sunrise. Pat and Cathy drove in our Chevrolet station wagon, while Carey and I followed in our Tempest. Later in the day, Pat would return with Carey to an apartment in Gainesville, where she would remain until she completed work on her master's degree in rehabilitation counseling. I would travel on in the other car to Charlotte, North Carolina, where I would begin my internship at Charlotte Memorial Hospital.

Carey's sweet, humorous observations along the way had offered me some diversion from my distressful thinking, but poor Pat—not only had she been denied the benefit of conversation, but she had watched helplessly as Cathy suffered a seizure only fifty miles from Tallahassee.

Now we were together at the Sunland Center for Retarded Children. The hospital administrator smiled compassionately as we signed the commitment papers. "Cathy will have everything she needs," he said assuringly. "We'll make certain of that."

The winsome expression of the silver haired executive filled me with the comforting feeling that Cathy would be cared for here. I reached out to take his hand in thanks before departing, but as our hands met, I suddenly froze.

Over the administrator's shoulder I'd seen Cathy struggling to be put down by the nurse holding her. Now, she was slowly crawling toward us. The administrator quickly whirled around, still grasping my right hand, to view what had caused my shocked expression.

Cathy worked her right side and then her left, determinedly moving her legs and arms to perform the awkward crawl she'd only recently mastered. Her little head rose and fell repeatedly as she tried to look up and bring her surroundings into focus.

"Pat," I whispered, nodding in Cathy's direction. Pat's hand rose to her lips as she gasped at the unprecedented feat.

A hush quickly fell over the room, as the few attendants and nurses present became aware of what was taking place. Only the slapping noise made by Cathy's small hands as she crawled broke the silence.

After five long years of praying and hoping and investing our time, money, and energy to make Cathy aware of us and the world around her, she'd waited until this day to finally react. I shook my head at the irony of it.

We watched Cathy's progress, still not knowing if she was indeed crawling to us. I wanted to stop this pitiful act. But hindering her would forever keep the question of Cathy's intentions in doubt.

Had Cathy, somewhere in an undamaged region of her tiny brain, solved the puzzle posed by these strange surroundings and faces and our tearful good-byes? Was it possible she could have figured all this out? Part of me wanted it to be so; the other part simply wanted to deny that any of this was happening.

Making the decision to give Cathy up was the hardest thing either Pat or myself had ever done. I'd been struggling all morning with my feelings, imploring God to assure me that we were making the right decision in turning Cathy over to the Sunland Center. Now, torn by my emotions, I felt perhaps I was being told I was indeed making the wrong choice.

Cathy continued on the course she had somehow set for herself until she had amazingly crawled the width of the twenty-foot-wide classroom to where we stood near the door. Pat, five months pregnant with our third child, wiped her eyes with her hands and knelt down, instinctively holding out her arms to Cathy.

A queer light flickered in Cathy's eyes as Pat pulled our daughter up into her arms; for a moment, I thought I detected some inner struggle by Cathy to emerge from behind the familiar vacant look and make contact.

No sooner had Pat gathered Cathy up, however, than our daughter began crying and twisting her body in an effort to be put down. She didn't recognize her mother after all.

I didn't see how I could bear another moment of this emotional roller coaster.

The hopes dashed so often before had cruelly reemerged as each slapping, uncoordinated movement brought Cathy closer to us. I had found myself thinking again that perhaps we could still make a go of caring for Cathy ourselves. Her condition could change. . . .

But we'd gone through it all so many times. In prior months, our greatest desire was to successfully nurture Cathy in our home. But as her seizures increased and her appetite diminished to nothing, that option faded.

We were convinced that Cathy had not formed any bonds whatsoever with us or derived any emotional nurturing from her family members. We were strangers in her blurred, confused world, despite all our efforts over the years to make contact. So it seemed, until now—the precise moment we were relinquishing the responsibility for her care to this institution.

Miraculously, we'd made it to this point. When we were the most vulnerable, our deepest needs had been met.

I'd come to realize that when I faced a crisis, I could best maintain my bearings by recounting previous dark moments when God had saved me from my vulnerabilities. I would also seek out the counsel and example of people like Pat, who possess the enviable inner strength to accept the burdens and tragedies of life.

From an awareness of God's mysterious and wonderful providence had sprung the strength—the only strength—I could rely on in times of difficulty. Yet, as often before, I found myself mired in doubt, wondering: *Will God's strength be there for me now?*

It was Pat to whom I turned as Cathy's crawl across the Sunland floor threatened to turn my world upside down again. I pulled her aside, anxiously wanting to make the right response to this unforeseen development.

"Pat, we have to decide what we're going to do and pray that it's the right decision," I said.

Pat reached for a tissue in her purse and dabbed the

tears from her eyes as she watched Cathy crawl back into the center of the classroom.

"We've already made our decision," she said solemnly. "Cathy can't be cared for at home. Her life will be less threatened here. Our decision has been made."

I knew those words were among the hardest Pat had ever spoken; it took all the courage she had to say them.

The Sunland administrator quietly left us and walked toward Cathy. He picked her up, kissed her on the forehead, and placed her in the arms of an attendant. Turning back toward us, he rested his hands on each of our shoulders.

"Cathy will be fine here," he said tenderly. "We'll see she gets the best care. And you know you're welcome to visit here at any time."

The administrator's words helped immensely, and we both expressed our appreciation for them. After hugging and kissing Cathy, we turned and began the difficult walk down several long corridors toward the main entrance. Cries of children mingled with our echoing footsteps as we made our way out. I tried to shut out the sounds, but I could not. Neither could I erase from my mind the look on Cathy's face as she knelt before us.

There were no words spoken as the three of us made our way to the cars. We leaned against the side of our station wagon, taking a moment to assimilate our emotions before saying good-bye.

I blew out a deep sigh. "You two be careful on the trip home," I said finally. Carey looked restless to get started. She didn't understand the meaning of this emotion-filled break in the parking lot.

"We will," Pat said quietly. She turned her reddened eyes toward me. "Call us when you get there, OK?"

I caught Pat looking a short distance across the lot at a car. . . . No, what was it? . . . A bumper sticker. In big red letters it read: "God Is My Co-Pilot."

At any other time this simply worded plastic strip

would have gone unnoticed or cast off, perhaps, as trite. But God used it to communicate a significant truth to us in our silent grief.

I hugged the two of them and said good-bye. We drove off from Sunland together and parted a short time later onto separate highways. At the crossroads, they waved, and I waved back.

I reflected on how drastically our family had changed in just a few short hours. This final parting of ways made me realize the fragility of all the relationships I held dear and the delicate nature of life itself. It didn't seem possible that we could withstand any more strain, any more heartache. My feelings of loss and loneliness were more profound than any I'd experienced since my time away from my family in the navy.

Nearly eleven hours had passed since leaving Tallahassee. Up ahead the sign read, "Charlotte—102 miles." I'd be home—although it wouldn't feel much like home without my family around me—in less than two hours.

I was bushed from the long trip. The fact that I would be sleeping on nothing but the mattress I carried in back until the movers arrived tomorrow was of little matter to me. I was just glad to be getting settled and starting my new job.

That'll be exciting, I tried to convince myself. *The new work will improve my whole outlook.*

➡ *But my God shall supply all your need according to his riches in glory by Christ Jesus* (Phil. 4:19, KJV).

➡ *Be not dismayed whate'er betide, God will take care of you* (C. D. Martin).

CHAPTER

DOUBLE GRIEF

It didn't take long to discover there was truth behind
the warning of friends that hospital internships are
notoriously difficult. Indeed, within several days of my
arrival at Charlotte Memorial Hospital I received
numerous fiery baptisms in the methods of treating a
wide range of problems, many of which were not
thoroughly covered in med school.

I was not alone, at least, in being a "new kid" on the
hospital floor. A number of interns, like me, had begun
their training at the hospital on the first of July. We
quickly drew together in a spirit of camaraderie, offering
one another mutual understanding and support.

When possible, we ate our meals together in the
cafeteria or spent time talking in the interns' lounge.
Most of the men were also young and married, with
small children. The painful difference between me and

the rest of them was that when they were through with work they had families to go home to.

After a couple of weeks, grumbling over the unpredictable rigors of hospital work became the dominant topic of our conversations. The complaints centered chiefly on the overnight periods spent on call, which kept the young interns away from their families.

"It never fails," one of them said at lunch one day after seeing the week's schedule. "I end up on call every time my boy has a ball game. I haven't seen him play in the last two."

With absolutely nothing pressing on my personal schedule, I gallantly volunteered to pull call duty for this young husband and father.

"You mean it?" he asked. "You sure you don't mind?"

"No, not at all," I replied. "My family isn't due here for another four weeks, so I haven't got anything better to do."

"Ross, you're a lifesaver," he said. "I'll make it up to ya. I really appreciate it."

Unlike some of my peers, I had little difficulty throwing myself into my hospital work. The busier my mind and the longer the hours, the less time I had to consider the loneliness I felt by not having a family around me.

Soon, I was pulling call duty for nearly all of my colleagues to allow these men to be with their families or to honor other commitments. At one point I found myself on call on three successive nights.

Without realizing it, I was disregarding my own well-being. Everyone was amazed at how long and hard I appeared to be able to function without sleep.

My only comfort during this time was talking to Pat over the phone. I called as much as our slight incomes would permit. We communicated the events of our days, offering what little consolation we could and dreaming of the time we could be a whole family once again.

Pat would say work on her master's degree was progressing well, and I spoke optimistically about my dream to be a medical missionary—a dream that was miraculously back on track.

One night, Pat sounded particularly down. She complained, "Being apart during this emotionally hard time is the last thing we need."

It was ironic, she said, that the master's program in which she had enrolled to deflect some of our family's financial burdens should become another kind of obstacle to our family life.

"I know it's hard," I commiserated with her. "But don't get down on yourself. My choice of careers has been the greatest reason we've led such a splintered existence in the last eight years.

"The navy and medical school were a strain on us all, and things are tough now, but we'll get through. You'll be finished down there before you know it."

On several occasions during these long-distance conversations Pat detected a weariness in my voice, but I sloughed it off. "A little extra call duty, that's all," I said.

I continued on with my work, staying up most nights on call, trying not to wonder how I would make it through this trying, empty period.

The phone rang one afternoon in the interns' room, just as I was washing up to go to dinner. I was scheduled to go on call that night for pediatrics.

"Dr. Campbell? Pediatrics," said a woman on the other line.

"Yes?"

"Listen, we're about to admit Nancy Flood with a case of klebsiella pneumonia," she said. "You know about Nancy, don't you?"

"The little girl with cystic fibrosis? Yes," I replied. "I'll be in the cafeteria if you should need me. I'm going to get some dinner before I go on."

The twelve-year-old girl, if I recollected properly, had

been admitted for klebsiella pneumonia more than twenty times. Later, when I checked her medical chart, I discovered I hadn't been off by much: There'd been twenty-eight admissions, in fact.

The difficult-to-treat disease is a common affliction of people suffering from the lung disease cystic fibrosis. Her antibiotic treatments had almost become routine in the pediatrics ward.

Each time she was admitted, the staff morbidly wondered if this would be her last treatment.

After dinner, I went to check on her.

"Hi, Nancy," I said with a smile. "Just couldn't stand to be away from us, huh? Well, I don't blame you. We're a fun crowd."

The frail child laughed lightly.

"The people here are the best friends I have," she said. Her thin face became serious. "But I sure wish I could get well."

I gazed into the beautiful, but dark-circled blue eyes of the little girl. Since I'd seen her last she'd lost a lot of weight. Her once shiny brown hair had lost its luster, and her hands, which she lifted off the bed to gesture briefly and wave to staff members, were little more than skin and bone.

"Nancy," I said. "We'll do our best to help you get well. When you come back the next time, I want it to be only to visit and say, 'Hello.' "

Nancy smiled between her labored breaths. "I like you, Dr. Campbell. Everyone's so nice to me here. Everybody wants me to get well, don't they?"

"You'd better believe it," said a nurse cheerfully as she walked up to change the girl's intravenous medication. "You'll feel brand new after you leave here."

The remainder of the night had been pretty uneventful. After several hours of watching television and reading in the doctors' lounge, I decided to turn in.

About two in the morning, the phone rang. It was

pediatrics calling to say Nancy's condition had dramatically deteriorated. Her temperature had shot up to 105 degrees, and her vital signs were erratic.

Leaping from my bed, I threw on my clothing and grabbed my stethoscope.

I knew something was wrong when I entered the room. Sadness was reflected in the faces of the team of intensive care nurses working with her.

"She's dying," one of the nurses said.

The little girl's respirations had slowed to one every twenty seconds. At 2:13 A.M., she was dead.

The entire staff was in a state of shock. I somehow stumbled back to the interns' room and collapsed onto the bed. All I could think of were the promises I'd made to her just hours before. She was my patient, my responsibility, and she was dead.

From deep within, I felt something rushing to the surface. I began to shake uncontrollably, and I burst into tears.

Loud, long groans accompanied my sobbing. I lay on the bed torn by remorse at the death of this child. With each convulsive movement and involuntary moan, I became convinced I was having a nervous breakdown.

I was petrified I would either receive another call or someone would enter the room and find me crying and moaning like a madman.

Several hours passed, but I still was unable to restrain my hysteria. I kept seeing in my mind the face of the dead girl. As I tried unsuccessfully to purge the image from my thoughts, her face dissolved into that of my own daughter, Cathy.

The images interchanged: First I saw Nancy's face, then Cathy's. And each time the image of Cathy's face entered my surging thoughts, it was the expression I'd seen when she'd crawled to her mother at the Sunland center.

Finally at 6:00 A.M., after nearly four hours of this tremendous outpouring of emotion, I began to gain control of myself. Despite the fact that I had not slept in virtually forty-eight hours, I somehow felt more refreshed than I had in a long time.

I knew that something very cleansing had happened.

Later, when I became familiar with psychological matters, I began to understand the meaning of my experience. Five years of grief, five years of struggling with Cathy and her problems, including the humiliation of her diagnosis and the frustration with our patterning sessions, had come out in those four hours.

The death of little Nancy had triggered the grief I felt for Cathy's symbolic death, which had occurred when we were forced to institutionalize her. The void created by Cathy's absence from us actually produced a more profound grief than had she actually died because we were denied a sense of finality to our separation.

At the time, I didn't know what grief was. I had the old-fashioned impression that men don't cry, that men are strong and don't give in to their emotions. Nor did I know how seriously I had placed my own health in jeopardy by refusing my body the rest it needed.

My experience in the interns' room that night in Charlotte did more than purge me of broken dreams, disillusionment, and bitterness, however; it also produced in me a vivid awareness of how deep, and often hidden, are the anguish and pain of parents who have children with problems. My compassion for these parents was among the reasons that later led me into the study of psychiatry, especially child psychiatry. I believe it was the motivation for taking the extra two years of training required for a fellowship in child psychiatry.

All parents of special children basically go through the same agony, my training has taught me. And I empathize with any who know that devastating pain. There are approaches to counseling that can help parents such as these, although for many it may seem at first that nothing can rectify their emotional damage.

I would later come to consider my entrance into psychiatry as a fulfillment of Paul's commandment in the first chapter of 2 Corinthians. He tells us there that helping others in their times of affliction is the business of all in Christ who have suffered. God's love and help is always present, but we are commanded to serve as his emissaries to the afflicted. By giving empathy and counsel, I would come to see, I could extend God's help to those who hurt.

▶ *Blessed be the God and Father of our Lord Jesus Christ, the Father of mercies and God of all comfort; who comforts us in all our affliction so that we may be able to comfort those who are in any affliction with the comfort with which we ourselves are comforted by God* (2 Cor. 1:3-7, NASB).

▶ *God often comforts us, not by changing the circumstances in our lives, but by changing our attitude towards them* (S. H. B. Masterman).

CHAPTER

9

PLANE MADNESS

With a determined burst of strength, I finally threw open my stubborn office window and thrust my head and shoulders outside as if I had emerged from being underwater. I found little relief. The still, sultry mid-morning air, seemingly layered upon itself, rivaled the heaviness of the jungle hospital's small, oppressive spaces. Only the shrill calls of distant tropical birds penetrated the outer stillness of the South American missionary base.

I looked at my watch and wiped a droplet of fallen perspiration from its face with my thumb. It was 9:35, but the steady crush of sick patients made it seem much later.

The familiar screeches of the jungle birds seemed to be drawing closer. The huge, ravenlike creatures quickly descended from overhead, landing in a line of trees at the rear of the hospital where they renewed the unwelcomed racket. I considered reclosing the window to spare myself all the noise, but I needed the fresh air more than the quiet.

Thus far this morning, there'd been the usual ailments to treat—cases of dysentery, influenza, and strep, plus a smashed thumb and a badly lacerated foot. I'd had to take X rays and even perform some minor dental work. After more than two hours of receiving these sick and injured people, the majority of whom were nationals, I was beginning to feel a little woozy myself.

I'm definitely not here for my own health, I reminded myself as I pulled away from the window to answer the phone.

"Dr. Campbell, this is Harry. You've got to come down to the hangar at once. Rachel's in one of the planes, and she's lost control of herself."

The voice of Harry Hillis, the director of this jungle base, was as frantic as any I'd ever heard. Momentarily, I thought he was jesting, which would have belied his usual retiring nature. But the tone in his voice was much too grave. He repeatedly spat out the words, "You've got to get down here right away."

"What do you mean she's lost control," I asked. "Is she trying to fly the thing?"

"No, no. She ran up to one of our pilots a short while ago demanding to be flown back to the States," he explained, practically out of breath.

"You're kidding?" I interjected.

"No. She has her luggage and she's sitting in a plane located near the runway. She's absolutely frantic. She says she can't stay here any longer. And she won't get out of the plane. You must get down here and talk to her."

"Has anyone else tried talking to her?" I asked.

"Of course," he replied. "Her husband and everyone else. But it hasn't done any good. Please hurry!"

"Harry, I can't leave my patients," I said with all the

forcefulness a short-term missionary doctor straight from
internship could muster. "I've got a waiting room full of
sick people. Treating them is more important than trying
to calm down a hysterical woman. Can't you people
work it out?"

"No. We've tried," he said, his voice cracking from
strain. "You've got to get down here right now!"

Finally, I relented. The director sounded so upset and
frightened of what the woman might do that I had no
choice other than to accept his judgment that this
was a major emergency. Besides, having just arrived
at the jungle outpost with my wife and two small
children several months before, I was trying to be as
accommodating as I could. I certainly wasn't in any
position to argue with the base director, no matter how
jumbled his priorities might seem.

"OK, Harry," I said. "I'll be there as soon as I can."

By this time, both of my nurses were standing inside
the doorway of my office, eyebrows raised and ears
perked for the news that had appeared so urgent over
the telephone.

"I've got to go to the base hangar," I said, pulling off
my lab coat. "It seems one of our missionaries has grown
very distraught and she's demanding to be flown home
to the States immediately."

"Gee, I wonder if we could go together," one of the
nurses said, giggling.

I handed her my stethoscope and looked anxiously
into the crowded waiting room of sick men, women, and
children.

"I'll be back as soon as I can. You two will just have to
make do. I hope this doesn't amount to anything."

I pushed the kick start of my little Honda scooter and
puttered off in a swirl of dust. Motorbikes were the only
means of ground transportation on base, which made
them valuable enough, but they were even more
desirable to those of us who valued the skin on our legs.

Anyone who walked long distances around the area invariably bore unsightly scars from the knees down— large, red welts created by insect bites that made even pretty legs look bad. For this trip, however, it was the speed of the motorbike, not the freedom it provided from insects, that made me glad to have it.

My thoughts kept pace with the swift-moving scooter as I traveled the approximate mile to the hangar. I considered myself a well-trained graduate of the University of Florida Medical School who had proven his skills in internship, so I usually felt little trepidation in offering my healing skills.

But I felt wholly unprepared for the task toward which I was speeding; it was unquestionably out of the realm of my healing arts. Having been a Christian for twelve years seemed to be the greatest credential I had going for me.

For the director and Rachel's husband, Walter, the natural response to this unexpected chain of events was simply to call the good base doctor and have him fix things. They were convinced it was a situation that called for quick, decisive, professional action. There was no denying I was all they had.

However, should my efforts end in failure, I was prepared to tell them there had been nothing in my studies of organic chemistry to show how a doctor could bring a jungle missionary to her senses. While I had received a brief emphasis on psychiatric care during my junior year of medical school, my knowledge in the field was minimal at best.

As I bounced along the bumpy road, I tried to prepare myself for the delicate job ahead. From what the director had described, I imagined Rachel to be literally pulling out her hair and banging her head against the cockpit. I tried to summon up some of the strategies I'd previously read or heard about for coaxing depressed individuals from despair and dark thoughts of suicide.

Rachel's demand to be flown to the U.S. in one of the outpost's Helio-Couriers was an indication to me of how irrational she was: All the base personnel knew the single engine planes only had a range of a few hundred miles.

It suddenly occurred to me that in my haste to depart the hospital, I had failed to bring along my medical bag, which, I dreaded to think, might be necessary if Rachel required sedation for her own protection.

It's just as well, I thought. *The ominous sight of a physician closing in with his black bag in tow might distress her even more.*

I was so deep in thought at this point that I had to swerve violently to miss a large rock lying along the uneven shoulder of the dirt road. The near-disaster rattled me.

I hoped it wasn't an omen of things to come.

After recovering my equilibrium, I began mulling over what I knew of the Jones family, which, unfortunately, was limited because of my brief tenure to date and the demands of their duties as Bible translators in a distant village. During brief social encounters with Rachel, I had found her to be a likable person with a sound faith. However, she was strong-willed and aggressive, personality traits that struck me as somewhat uncharacteristic for the wife of a Bible translator.

Through discussions with other missionaries, I had learned that while the particular tribe assigned to the Jones couple was more civilized, culturally speaking, than other Amazonian peoples, it was also more hostile. This, understandably, had posed a formidable and dangerous challenge for the translators.

The middle-aged couple lived with their four children at the jungle headquarters in one of the nicer residences—a sturdy, comparatively roomy structure at the other end of the outpost from us. However, the couple spent a small portion of each month on base, choosing instead to push ahead with their work in the village. When they did check in at home it was only to obtain supplies, consult with fellow translators, and see how their children were doing in the base school—a testimony, I thought, to their Christian commitment and strong-willed natures.

And yet, things had not gone well with their translation of the New Testament. In fact, the married team possessed the unhappy distinction of having had the least success of any set of translators on base. What's more, they'd already been at it for twelve years.

What was most obvious about Walter and Rachel, I felt, was that they were Christians and dedicated missionaries. Persecution, hostility, meager funds, isolation, and hard work constitute the diets of missionaries, I'd always thought. These things take their toll on some people, I'd concluded, but not on missionaries—not on sound, loving, courageous Christian people like the Joneses seemed to be.

I couldn't see any reason for Rachel to crack. *It must be frustrating work, though,* I conceded. *Even the best missionaries would get a little stir-crazy after almost twelve years in the jungle.*

I rounded one last bend in the sun-baked road and caught sight of the wood and aluminum open-air hangar. Six or eight people were huddled about fifty yards away from the hangar—a "safe" distance from the Helio-Courier single engine aircraft.

It was nearly ten o'clock, and the scorching tropical sun had already begun to make things uncomfortable. My first concern was for the physical well-being of Rachel, who, presumably, was still holed up inside the plane; I gathered as much from the exasperated looks on the faces of the director, her husband, and the other people who had assembled to help.

I pulled alongside the hangar and parked my vehicle. The group, led by the director, moved earnestly toward me as I pocketed my keys and slapped at my trousers to remove the dust. As I strode toward them, I sensed a ripple in the expressions of the group's members. Everyone still looked concerned and a little stunned, but there was now also some relief on their faces.

Everyone, that is, except Walter, Rachel's husband. His expression distinguished him immediately from the others. It was the look of a man who was apt at any moment to dive into a hole or shinny up a mango tree, whichever happened to be closest.

I suddenly was struck with the feeling that a Christian—namely, me—had been found for the lions' den, or that the explosives expert had arrived and everyone could breathe easier now that the time bomb was about to be defused. I tried to hide my annoyance at being put under such pressure.

"Has anything else happened?" I asked upon reaching the group.

"No. We, uh, haven't bothered her," the director said, looking sympathetically at Walter.

"She keeps shouting to be flown home every time someone tries to speak to her. We offered to pray with her, but this only made her more agitated. I know she's getting hot in there." He arched his thin eyebrows and gave me the kind of pathetic look one gets from a helpless child or puppy. "See what you can do."

He edged me slightly away from the group.

"She's threatened suicide," he whispered solemnly.

Walter joined us. "Thanks for coming, Ross," he offered feebly.

"I'll do what I can," I said as amicably as I could. "I don't know if I can do any more than you've already done."

I spun away from the cluster of hopeful faces and began to walk in the direction of the Helio-Courier.

Crossing the stretch of hardened earth that served as the base's runway, my gaze fixed on the small plane twenty yards or so before me. For a moment, I envisioned myself as the gullible, unsuspecting soul sometimes portrayed in literature and in film—a Charlie Chaplin type. At the admonition of his cohorts, one of these Trusting Toms predictably accepts a daring assignment that everyone but that poor soul knows is fated for disaster. I quickly turned around to see if anyone in the group was watching with amusement as I made my progress toward the plane. They weren't.

Of course not, I thought, shutting out the idea I'd been made a patsy. *These people really need me to do something. I've got to try.*

I resolutely strode to the aircraft's left side, thinking Mrs. Jones would be seated to the right of the undivided seat inside the plane. After wiping my moist palms on my shirt, I grasped the handle bolted on the plane's body and pulled myself up by stepping on the foot pads beneath the door.

Instinctively, I tilted back my head to avoid coming into contact with any projectiles thrown in my direction. Rising gingerly, I reached a point where I could peer into the tiny window on the pilot's side.

Through the clear plastic panel located just below the window, my eyes met a face glaring up at me.

"Hi," I said sheepishly.

The woman's expression remained unchanged. I knew she could hear me, because the windows had been pushed open to permit what little breeze there was to flow through the cramped cockpit. But she made no effort to speak.

"How ya doin'?" I asked, feeling a little awkward that she no doubt read my purpose in coming. "What are you doing in the plane?" was all I could think to say next.

The face of the attractive brown-haired woman was smudged and moist; her dark brown eyes were rimmed with red. Straightening up from her slouched position she inhaled unevenly, as though preparing to speak or cry, but only continued to glower at me. Although she was considerably more calm than I had expected—a result, I surmised, of being left alone for a while—it was apparent she was still very distressed.

She clutched her purse and a shredded tissue with one hand, while struggling with the other hand to push aside two pieces of luggage next to her on the seat and edge away from me. How had she found the strength to lift the heavy luggage into the plane in the first place?

"What do you want?" she said finally with an angry scowl.

"I'm here to help you," I replied calmly.

She looked away and sighed heavily. Her chin dropped slightly and then she turned back toward me.

"Then get me out of this place right now," she hissed deliberately in a low, harsh voice as if each word possessed a bad taste.

I was shocked by her hostility.

"Can you fly this plane?" she asked tersely. "I want to go home. I cannot stay another day in this God-forsaken hole."

In a whiny, almost childlike tone, tinged with desperation and anger, she began telling me that nothing was going right. As I had suspected, the translation work in her tribe was doing poorly due to growing hostility on the part of the tribespeople. She'd interpreted this display of resentment, which was rare among South American tribes, as a negative commentary on her and her husband's abilities.

"We don't have any business being here," she sobbed. "I can't believe we were so stupid to think we could make any progress among these . . . animals!"

As Rachel bared her tormented soul, she expressed the belief that the couple's failures were the result of somehow having "fallen from God's grace."

"God's just given up on us, and I don't blame him," she cried. "And I don't want to be here any more than he wants me here. I'm through with this place!"

The growing frustration of trying to raise four children in such severe conditions, she continued, accounted for the final blow that had pushed her to the brink of despair.

"Please get me out of here right now," she sobbed.

The sudden shift from her concern for her children back to her demand to be freed of responsibility indicated just how impaired her thinking had become.

"Rachel, I would like to get you back home right now, but it's not something we can do just like that." I snapped my fingers for effect.

I hoped my glibness would not ignite her rage; it didn't, so I continued.

"This little plane couldn't even get you to the capital, much less the U.S.," I asserted. "You know that, don't you?"

Her stony expression remained unchanged.

"And what can you do after you get to the capital? You haven't got any reservations to fly home from there."

I could see from the tears welling up in her eyes that she was on the verge of another outburst, so I spoke quickly.

"But I'll do everything I can to make arrangements for your trip home. Just give me the time to do that."

I regretted making this promise before I knew the outcome of our talk, but I was playing for time. I felt if she could calm down and rest, her frantic, compulsive demands to leave would pass, and then we could begin trying to understand the source of her distress.

She nodded her head jerkily.

"OK," she agreed, obviously dissatisfied with having to compromise. "OK. But you've got to promise you'll make reservations immediately. You've got to get me out of here today."

She pushed her red face closer to the window's opening.

"You promise?"

"I'll do my best," I said, trying to avoid a direct answer. "Now let's get you out of here and back home where you can rest."

"I don't want to see anybody, and I don't want to talk to anybody," she intoned as she began collecting her belongings.

"That's fine," I said. I was relieved her anger had subsided and things had progressed this far. The less contact she had with people, permitting her to rest and settle her thoughts, the better.

I jumped backwards from the wing, landing clumsily in the dust and twisting my ankle in the process.

"Ouch!" I yelped. I hopped around the plane on my good foot, trying to accommodate her exit on the other side with my outstretched arms. She showed no concern for my pain.

"I can make it," she said sourly. My resentment flared, and I realized how thankful I was to be married to Pat and not to this woman. Recognizing the blessing of this reality even seemed to bring relief to my aching foot.

She jerked her luggage through the tiny angular door and dropped each piece on the ground. Hanging her purse on one arm, she scrambled to the ground and pulled her luggage toward her.

"Here, let me help," I volunteered as graciously as my pain and resentment permitted.

"I can manage," she muttered.

The most pitiful sight any of our onlookers probably ever witnessed was that of this emotionally drained woman dragging her luggage in the dust and heat with a hot, sweating, short-term missionary doctor hobbling beside her.

As she headed in the direction of her home, roughly two hundred yards away, I hurried as best I could in the opposite direction to intercept Walter, the director, and the others.

"She needs to be left alone to rest," I informed them.

"I'm going to take her home. We'll decide later what we can do to help her."

Walter nodded thoughtfully and breathed deeply. His face revealed a guarded sense of relief.

"Thanks, Ross," he said gratefully. "I don't know what you said, but you must have worked a miracle. She was really determined to fly out of here today."

"Well, I'm just thankful she didn't hurt herself and that I didn't have to sedate her," I said. "I didn't work any miracles. She just needed a neutral person to talk calmly to her. That's all we can do at this point, I guess.

"Just pray now that God will help her rest, because she's exhausted. We're not out of the woods yet. We'd better help her get home."

"Thanks, Ross," the director said. His trembling hands and shaky voice told me he was still a little rattled. "I'm sorry we had to take you from your work." He looked down at my foot. "And I'm sorry you hurt yourself."

"It's OK. Glad to help." I winced in pain as I turned to join Walter, who was already hustling to catch up with his wife.

Rachel at last allowed me and her husband to relieve her of her bags. The three of us walked silently through the thick foliage, following the dirt path that led to their residence.

"Here they come," a child's voice shouted in the distance. A flurry of footsteps followed. "They're coming home."

After managing to get Rachel to bed, I sat down in a chair in the living room to nurse my ankle. Walter looked at me anxiously, as if I had some wisdom to offer him.

I didn't really know what to say, except that his wife needed a great deal of rest.

"I'm sorry about your ankle," he said. "Can I get you anything, some ice maybe?"

"Some iced water would be good . . . for my mouth," I said, smiling.

As he retrieved the water, I could hear him in the kitchen hurrying the children out the back door to play. When he returned, he handed me the glass and sat down on the couch near my chair.

"Rachel needs a lot of rest," I pointed out again. "She needs to stay in bed, even if that means bringing her meals into the bedroom." He nodded quietly.

"Is she going to need some help . . . professional help?" he asked. He showed obvious difficulty in speaking the words, as if he were uttering some sacrilege.

"Yes. That's certainly in order," I replied. "But I'm not really trained to counsel her. I wish I were. I'll certainly do my best to get to the source of her feelings and help in that way. I strongly suggest you consider diminishing your work load . . . or . . . turning over your duties to someone else."

Horror crossed his face. "Oh. We can't do that. We're really beginning to make progress. Introducing new translators would destroy everything we've done. We'll pray. We'll pray that God will permit us to continue."

"I'll pray, too," I said. "We'll all pray. But consider the needs of your wife, too, Walter."

Making my way slowly down the dirt pathway back to my motorbike near the hangar, I grappled with what I could do to help Rachel. I felt so unequipped, so ill-prepared to offer any solutions.

I grieved that my medical training didn't permit me to promote the healing of this missionary's invisible but very real illness. To be sure, I was equally saddened that Rachel had turned a deaf ear to the Christian counsel and prayers of her peers.

Later that night at home, as the dust of the day's unexpected events began to clear, I felt left holding a mixed bag of emotions—disillusionments, emptiness, sadness, perplexity—and a question that seemed unanswerable: "What can I do to help you, Rachel?"

Four years of medical school and a one-year internship had provided me with numerous skills; I'd even become fairly proficient in basic dentistry and radiology during supplemental training sessions between classes. But despite all this training, I felt wholly inadequate to tackle Rachel's problem from a professional standpoint. How I wish I knew then what I do now.

Nevertheless, leaning on the nine short weeks of psychiatric training I had received in medical school, I proceeded with marriage counseling for the Joneses at Walter's request. Rachel's shame and humiliation over her drastic behavior immediately surfaced during the sessions. These feelings grew steadily as she moved out into the base community and sought to renew contact with her friends.

The sessions constituted little more than lay counseling on my part. It was because of the Jones' commitment to their marriage, to each other, and to Christ, rather than anything I did, that Rachel's frayed emotions began to heal.

I wondered initially if Rachel's difficulty was being posed by some internal imbalance, or if there was possibly some outside force affecting her misery. Was there some truth, some hidden method, that might reverse her sudden, inexplicable turnaround? What caused the paralyzing pressure and fear that hit her every morning when she awoke? And how might she be freed from it?

I hurt right along with Rachel, her husband, and her children. But in time, the couple showed amazing strength and adeptness in repairing their shattered attitudes toward their work and their relationships with Christ and each other.

No sooner had I completed counseling the Joneses than I became deluged with other base employees suffering from emotional and psychological problems. Again, I was expected to deal with these problems, and again, they proved well beyond the realm of my expertise. Some of these missionaries actually had to return to the U.S. for further in-depth help.

Neither Pat nor myself saw much of the Joneses from that point on, as they headed back out to their tribe and reinitiated their translating work. We would be leaving ourselves for the States after our term was up in a few months.

But we never forgot Rachel. From time to time, we would remember to say a prayer for her and her family and wonder what progress was being made by them in the bush. When I returned to the U.S., I discovered that my experience with her and others in the extreme conditions of the isolated missionary outposts had planted seeds in my thinking: I would enroll in psychiatric training and get some answers. Maybe I could unlock the doors that stood between people like Rachel and their happiness and spiritual perspective.

Midway through the writing of this book, we received a packet of material from the mission society with which we had served in South America. In it were assorted sheets of information similar to those we'd seen before on numerous occasions. But this particular collection bore a special little newsletter that quickly caught our attention.

In the newsletter was the announcement that the Joneses had—after some twenty-seven years of diligent work—at last completed the translation of the New Testament into the language of their assigned tribe in the summer of 1984. Furthermore, the information stated, the couple had achieved a powerful Christian impact in the tribal village and the surrounding region.

The arrival of this good news could not have been more timely. Its value to us was not seen simply as a means to conclude this story, but as an affirmation of

God's unceasing goodness and undergirding strength on behalf of those people who take God's call in their lives seriously.

▶ *I have fought the good fight, I have finished the course, I have kept the faith; in the future there is laid up for me the crown of righteousness, which the Lord, the righteous Judge, will award to me on that day . . .* (2 Tim. 4:7, 8, NASB).

▶ *We need to learn to set our course by the stars and not by the lights of every passing ship* (Omar Bradley).

CHAPTER

LOST OVER THE JUNGLE

"Boy, this equipment," I muttered in frustration.

"Is there anything we can do to bring up a better signal?" I hollered back to the attendant in the radio shack. "Like reposition the antennae or check the wiring?"

"Nah," he said with a shrug. "It's just a weak signal. It's originating from a good way off."

My face was practically touching the radio speaker as I crouched forward to hear the message above the hiss of static.

"Please repeat," I called into the mike. "Repeat your last transmission."

This link by ham radio was all that our missionaries in the remote Amazonian villages had in the case of a medical emergency. We short-term medical workers at the other end of the radio provided what counsel we could when they or any villagers required medical treatment. In the event of problems I could not handle by radio, one of the three base pilots and myself would set off for the village.

For five minutes I'd been struggling to understand this call for help with no success.

Finally, the static subsided long enough for several phrases to get through. "TB epidemic . . . we need medicine . . . an outbreak of tuberculosis in the Tamarani village . . ."

"That's the Tamarani missionary," I said. "Sounds like he's got a spread of TB on his hands.

"OK, we're on our way," I said loudly into the microphone, not knowing whether or not the translator had heard me. I turned to the radio shack technician. "Listen, see what you can do to improve this signal, OK? We need to let these people know we're coming."

"Right, Ross." He nodded. "I'll do my best."

I hurried outside to my motorbike and puttered off in the direction of the hangar. When I arrived, the only person on duty was Dennis Springer, a good-looking, rawboned base pilot. He was working on the engine in one of our two Helio-Courier aircraft. Grease and perspiration covered his unclad, well-tanned arms and torso.

"Dennis!" I yelled. "We've got an outbreak of TB in the Tamarani village. We need to fly medicine over there right away."

We had to get a move on. I glanced over my shoulder at the afternoon sun. It was already 1:30. We needed to be in and out of the village well before sundown. It was December 31, and I didn't want to be late for the New Year's Eve social planned for all of the base personnel tonight at our home.

In a short time, the two of us lifted from the base runway into a cloudless afternoon sky. Our destination was a remote Indian village located two hundred miles south of the main missionary base.

I had made many similar runs with Dennis, not to mention the other two base pilots, during my five months as a short-term medical missionary. I truly looked forward to the picturesque breaks these little hops over the Amazonian jungles afforded from my hectic routine on base.

Two and a half hours later, we dropped onto the village runway without incident.

"Thank goodness," the missionary said with relief when we emerged from the plane. "I didn't think I'd gotten through to you."

"Yeah, that was terrible reception," I said, as we began unloading our supplies. "It's always bad in the afternoon."

"Has something to do with the atmosphere heatin' up," Dennis interjected.

We walked the short distance to the village and set about examining the more severely ill members of the one-thousand-member tribe. We recorded our findings and spent the remainder of our time instructing the tribal authorities in the use of the drugs we had brought.

Dennis was rounding up supplies across from me in the mud-walled hut that had served as our temporary clinic when he suddenly stopped and grimaced.

"Hey, we're taking too much time," he said, raising up from his work. "We gotta get out of here. It's"—he held his watch close to his face to see it in the pale light—". . . it's almost six o'clock! Where did the time go?"

We hurried to collect our things, said our good-byes, and hustled through the tall grass to the runway.

Our plane lurched rapidly into the airspace above the Tamarani village and rose effortlessly with Dennis's guidance over the thicket of palm and mango trees at the far end of the landing strip. We'd quickly loaded our supplies and notebooks, as well as the pair of superbly crafted hammocks the Tamarani people had given us in appreciation of our work.

It was getting late, and we had a two-and-a-half-hour

trip back to the base. We'd shrugged off remaining in the village for the night because of our pressing schedules and the New Year's social we wanted to attend. Now I wasn't so sure we had made the right decision.

Pilots in Amazonia most fear getting caught by darkness while flying because there are essentially no navigational aids in the jungle; the landing strips are only primitive runways roughcast out of the jungle, and navigational lights are nonexistent. Consequently, an airplane caught aloft at night is in extreme danger. The worst thing that could happen is for an airborne party to crash into an overgrown, unexplored part of the jungle and never be heard from again.

We climbed steadily, our backs plastered to the thinly cushioned seat rests, until we reached our cruising altitude. It was now late evening, and twilight was fast closing in—as was a bank of storm clouds behind us.

Great, I thought, disheartened. *All we need is a thunderstorm.*

In front of us, though, was a limitless firmament of deep azure blue, its hue intensified by the tropical sun now beginning to set to our left. Mottled clouds near the western horizon had been set afire by the radiant, sinking sun.

The vast, unspoiled splendor of the tropical forests that lay between the two tributaries of the Amazon was like nothing I had ever seen. At a normal cruising altitude, the lush jungle floor below appeared to be an immeasurable green carpet, running in all directions as far as the eye could see.

The jungle's formless heights, decorated by the flowering pink and crimson tops of mahogany and cinnamon trees, often produced interesting patterns from a distance. At many points, you'd see the jungle's surface broken by twisting streams and small rivers, the source of life for the region's wild creatures. From my breathtaking vantage point, I could see how the rivers sometimes wound back onto themselves, creating small lakes like the one upon which our base was located.

But tonight I was unable to enjoy the magnificent beauty that lay before us. Until now, the short flights during my medical missionary work had given me the feeling that I was a part of a romantic adventure. Now, sitting on an extremely uncomfortable seat next to Dennis as we barreled headlong into a darkening sky, I had a completely different sensation.

The amber-colored jungle sun was nearly below the horizon's hazy rim. With the death of the last rays of sunlight, my hopes of finding a proper flight course home before nightfall began to evaporate.

As darkness fell over the luxuriant expanse below, and the once brilliant streaks of pink and orange turned ashen in color, the reality of our misguided adventure began to take hold. I looked out my tiny window, hoping to see stars in the heavens, but the swift-moving bank of clouds had obliterated their twinkling light. There was nothing beautiful or moving or comforting about this nocturnal scene.

Soon there was absolutely no more visible light, except for the artificial glow of the plane's instrument panel that created eery patterns on my partner's tightened features. Our nightmare had begun.

"Ross, if you've ever prayed, you'd better do it now," Dennis shouted over the roar of our airplane's single engine. "We're running out of time." He stared straight ahead, nervously chewing at a corner of his lower lip.

As I sensed his anxiety, I felt the pace of my heart quicken.

He worked feverishly with his right hand, twisting the knobs of the on-board radio and calling into the hand-held transmitter at each new setting to raise a signal from our base. He finally turned the task over to me and fell back in his seat, frustrated and obviously worried.

At that moment I would have given anything to hear an intelligible sound through the annoying, empty crackle of static on the radio. Both of us knew, however, that we were still too far from the base to receive an adequate signal. The approaching storm no doubt posed an additional obstacle to our reception.

The loneliness I began to experience high in the chilled Amazonian night air was the greatest I had ever known.

To say the ten-year-old, short-takeoff-and-landing, single engine (STOL) aircraft was modestly equipped would be a generous description. Planes of this sort were once favored for clandestine U.S. military operations in Southeast Asia; therefore, they possessed only the barest accoutrements. Their intended capacity was a maximum of six people and a limited amount of cargo.

The small, unpressurized, uninsulated, and unair-conditioned cabins of the base's two planes were fitted with two narrow seats for the pilot and one passenger. The rear portion carried a small mattress and a blanket, which were folded up and stowed when they were not in use.

Outwardly, the planes' aluminum, unpainted exteriors gave the appearance that they were little more than sheet metal held together with bars of steel. Thanks to the base aviation crew, who kept the aircraft routinely checked and well-maintained, the planes were quite airworthy.

But it was decidedly not the lap of luxury into which I had strapped myself for this return trip home. With night having fallen and the loud drone of the engine filling my ears, our plane more appropriately became for me a roaring death chariot with a propeller.

As my anxiety rose, so did my anger. I was intent on laying the blame for the unforgivable miscalculation of time upon Dennis alone. My fair, reasonable side kept telling me both Dennis and I had neglected to keep track of time during our afternoon at the village. But I didn't want to believe it.

The mission had given Dennis the task of charting the region and making maps. He, therefore, had an uncommon knack for reading landmarks in the terrain below and using them to ascertain directions and distances. His ability to do this, however, hinged on being able to see what was around him.

I agonized over the fact that our plane was so small and so slow that daylight had slipped away from us and there was nothing we could do about it. *If only I could turn back time,* I thought. *If only God would.*

The absence of stars further complicated matters. We had a magnetic compass; but with no other means of guidance, it was clear that Dennis and I were becoming more and more disoriented on this miserable night journey.

Assuming we were destined for the worst, I struck up an inner dialogue of self-recrimination. *How could I have been so stupid as to have ignored the time? How could I have been so careless?*

These thoughts, of course, only served to depress and anger me further.

I looked over every once in a while to observe Dennis's tense face, and each time his expression remained unchanged.

Finally, the anger grew within me to the point where I blamed God. *Here I am doing God's work, extending myself to the limit for him, and he's letting this happen. Doesn't he care about what we're doing for him?*

My thoughts momentarily drifted back to the base where our families were. By this time, Pat would be making last-minute preparations for the New Year's Eve social at our house.

We were living in a small wooden structure with

another family, which, like ours, had two children. A paper-thin wall stood as the only barrier between their spaces and ours. Neither family could help being aware of every joy, pain, disagreement, spanking, crying tantrum, angry outburst, or intimate moment of the other—except when it rained; then, the clatter created by the furious fall of raindrops on our flimsy tin roof prevented us from hearing anything.

But we had tried to count our blessings. We had running water—although it was always cold and required boiling to remove impurities—and we had enough food to eat—things like mangoes, yucca, papaya, fish, and beef, all of which had to be soaked in iodine to kill off tropical parasites and disease. A kerosene stove heated our food and a tiny kerosene refrigerator chilled it. While these were decidedly humble accommodations, they were not nearly as austere as the thatched adobe hut homes of the base missionaries who lived in the tribes. They built them, they said, so they might identify more readily with the Indians.

So, life on the jungle base was difficult. Pat especially had a tough job. In addition to running a household in these adverse conditions, she had been assigned to teach kindergarten at the base school. All of these things had amassed to place a terrible strain on her. But the thought that haunted me most at this time was not that I had dragged Pat to this missionary outpost, but that I was on the verge of making her a widow.

Suddenly, I thought of Carey and David. How could I leave Carey, who was only nine years old? She was a mature, happy child who handled new situations well. But she was also a sensitive child. What would losing her father do to her?

And how would David, our third child, who was fifteen months old, grow up properly without his father's guidance? My relationship with him had been much closer on the mission field than it would have been in the States. One advantage in running the mission hospital, although the work was exhausting and time-consuming, was the absence of medical or board meetings, training lectures, and the other customary activities that would have preoccupied me back home. This left time for David and the rest of my family.

My anguish deepened as I thought about my wife and children and the happiness I derived from them.

Dennis and I had been looking forward to the New Year's Eve celebration at the base. The social at my house had frequently popped up in conversation as we performed our medical duties earlier in the day. This was to be an exciting event, attended not only by the missionaries and their families, who hailed from many countries, but by a number of the nationals who lived near the base.

It was no longer the New Year's Eve festivities, however, that dominated our thoughts as we proceeded deeper into an unmarked, abyssal sky. Our plane had been supplied with just enough gasoline to carry us over the round-trip to and from the village. Staying aloft, then, for much longer than the planned time it would take us on the return leg of our trip was out of the question.

I gazed at my watch and then glanced at the slowly descending needle on the plane's fuel gauge. Exasperated, I let my head fall back against the seat. It seemed certain we'd have to try some sort of emergency landing in this undeveloped region.

The two of us had spoken little for several minutes. The incessant, high-pitched blare of the plane's engine forced us to shout to be heard, and neither of us felt like using the energy to do so. When we did speak, our communication was terse and businesslike. The noise made it almost impossible to think clearly, let alone pray.

I looked over at Dennis, and recalled all that we had been through together. I knew little about his background, except that he and his wife Ruth were farm kids from Indiana. I had delivered their fourth child with some difficulty, due to a painful complication that had arisen during Ruth's pregnancy.

Throughout the course of Ruth's extremely painful ordeal, I grew to respect her greatly. Her excruciating pain notwithstanding, she had refused any medication during delivery for fear it would slow the child's respirations and endanger its life.

The abnormal contractions produced by Ruth's complication had sent me scurrying to the base ham radio set for help. There I was able to contact an old friend who was an obstetrician practicing in Charlotte, North Carolina. On the basis of my description, he diagnosed the problem and made valuable suggestions.

Even after the problem had been identified, Ruth still remained committed to delivering without sedation. I was amazed and inspired by her courage. But the point came when I had to insist she accept the morphine. Lacking the equipment to handle serious obstetric complications, it was absolutely crucial that we proceed with the obstetrician's recommendations. I told her the pain she was experiencing could result in premature uterine contractions that could affect the baby.

Finally, she relented and later, with Dennis's assistance, I presented the couple with a beautiful new addition.

That incident had demonstrated how valuable Dennis could be in a pinch. One of the things I admired so much about him was that he was a man of instant decision. He had the uncanny knack of always knowing what to do in a time of crisis. During his wife's pregnancy, he had sensed that something was wrong and had picked her up and carried her to the delivery table at exactly the right moment.

His decisiveness and sheer physical strength had also proved valuable on another occasion. A flooded river in the jungle was preventing a mission party from carrying

its supplies to the opposite bank. While we all stood
around pondering our next move, Dennis had waded in
and begun transporting our goods through the river's
strong current.

Time after time, this ruggedly built pilot, determined
to squarely face problems and persevere, proved himself
to be a vessel of God's provision in this remote region.
He told me several times that it was his "wonderful
relationship" with God that empowered him with a sense
of knowing what to do at the right time.

Left to these thoughts, I momentarily regained
confidence that we would somehow overcome the
problems posed by this dark, treacherous flight. But my
feelings of gloom and anger would not go away. This
time, I knew Dennis had his work cut out for him.

I tried not to give any indication of my frustration,
although I felt as if I would scream at any moment. More
and more my anger shifted from Dennis and myself to
God, whom I felt had abandoned two earnest servants.

In between despairing thoughts and bitter darts cast
up at God, I feebly prayed that God would ignore my
lack of faith and permit us to locate some mark of
civilization to serve as a reference point and facilitate
our landing.

Almost two hours had passed since we left the village,
according to my watch. I clenched my fists and closed
my eyes as I heard the plane's engine sputter briefly.

"We're going down," I muttered defeatedly, engulfed
in fear. Dennis didn't hear me. "We're going down."

Suddenly, Dennis gasped. "I think I see a light!"

My eyes popped open and my heart began to race. I
intently peered into the shroud of night, moving my
head from side to side as I looked.

"Where?" I asked excitedly. "Where is it?"

"Look," he urged, nodding ahead. Then he pointed.
"There it is."

I desperately searched the darkness in the direction

Dennis had pointed. What seemed so plain to him still escaped my vision.

I prayed he wasn't hallucinating. With my face almost touching the windshield, I finally perceived a tiny pinprick of light. My spirits soared.

"I see it!" I shouted. "Yeah, I see it!"

I turned to look at my partner. As he glanced back, I saw a big grin appear on his face. I smiled back, feeling so happy I wanted to hug him.

We dropped to roughly five hundred feet and closed in on the light. The area lit by the flickering glow was fairly wide, but not so wide that it could aid our landing in unfamiliar jungle territory. We fervently hoped the light was man-made and that nearby was a village with friendly people and a landing strip.

Passing directly over the light, we saw it was in fact emanating from a campfire in a small village. A few thatched huts were visible in the considerable light cast by the fire, but no people could be seen. The village setting was unfamiliar to me.

"Where's the landing strip?" I muttered impatiently under my breath.

My fear mounted again as we failed to glimpse an area in the jungle brush where we might land. I settled back in my seat and began to prepare for the worst once more.

But as I turned to Dennis, I saw there was nothing resembling dejection on his face. He looked hopeful.

"You know," he suddenly blurted out, "I'm not sure, but I think that's San José. According to the map, there should be a tiny landing strip just north of here."

"Come on, baby," I whispered. "Get us outta this mess."

Dennis sensed I was sharing in his small surge of hope and suddenly became more talkative. Shouting, he informed me that because of the limited extent of our vision it would be impossible to tell if a landing strip existed in the heavy vegetation unless he dropped the plane down to a level just below the treetops.

The term *landing strip* is very loosely used in this barely civilized region. These strips are not asphalt or cement runways, but cleared paths in the wilderness not much wider than the wingspan of a STOL plane.

The airstrips were usually fashioned by tribespeople with the help of missionaries. Some were better than others. But none of them were totally safe.

Our pilots were among the best aviators in the world. But no one was so adept at landing and taking off that those short strips cluttered by huge stumps, logs, and cows didn't pose sizable hazards. Collisions with cows and logs, in fact, had been the primary cause of previous crashes by base pilots.

"I can only make one approach to where I think there might be a landing strip," he said. "If it's not there, we'll just have to hit the trees and take our chances."

He blinked hard and took a deep breath.

"Do you want to try, or do you want to keep on toward the base? Our fuel is low."

If we attempted a crash landing, we probably had better than a fifty-fifty chance of surviving. And if we did survive, we could only hope that the nearby Indians would be friendly to us until we were picked up by base personnel. The way I saw it, the low level of our fuel was pretty much going to decide things for us anyway. We could either crash-land here, with a village not too far away, or attempt to land in a more remote spot.

"It'll be like finding a needle in a haystack, won't it?" I asked.

"Yeah, sort of," Dennis replied. "But I really think I have a pretty good shot at hitting it."

"Well, let's go in, then," I answered back, praying silently that whatever airstrip we were fortunate enough to locate would be one where the villagers took great pride in their work.

"I'm going down," Dennis announced, flicking on his landing lights. He inched the controls forward to lower the plane's flaps.

I knew that Dennis was going to have to be right on the strip before he could see it. I felt my heart pounding in my throat. I held my breath as he began his sharp angle of descent in the direction where he thought the airstrip lay.

"Brace yourself," he stated calmly as he lowered the flaps.

I tensed my body for an impact as we dropped toward the trees. But the anticipated smack didn't happen; instead, we began skimming across the jungle treetops.

From this unusual perspective, the dense foliage of the trees appeared as a frondescent sea. The plane dropped still lower.

Without warning, Dennis shoved the controls forward and we plummeted over a rim of clustered branches into a yawning, darkened gap. The plane's strong beams of light shot down into the void. For a moment it seemed as if we had found a bottomless pit.

In an instant, there it was! An airstrip right in front of us! The scraggy strip wouldn't have looked any better if it had been LaGuardia International Airport.

At a level of about thirty feet above the landing strip, we could see numerous stumps amid the tall bunchgrass below. Because of the limited extent of our vision, Dennis was forced to make a rapid, almost acrobatic descent. The unexpected move took my breath away.

Quickly he inched the plane down, seeking a path most devoid of stumps. We touched ground.

A series of vigorous bumps followed, but with each bump I let out a sigh of relief.

We were down with only ten yards of remaining airstrip to spare. Had we dropped a second or two later, we would be picking splinters out of ourselves for the remainder of the night—or worse.

Dennis whooped like a kid. "Praise God!" he shouted.
"Absolutely," I sighed.

My legs felt like columns of jelly as I pulled myself
through the small door of the cockpit and clambered to
the ground. The firm earth felt wonderful beneath my
feet.

The sudden silence after hours of the nerve-wracking
bray of the plane's engine was eery. But we were at once
enveloped in a cacophony of jungle sounds as we left
the plane. I was not annoyed by the audible night play
of creatures, however. Even the occasional squawks of
jungle birds were music to my ears.

The sounds of life are good, I thought. *It's good to be
a survivor.*

We collected a few supplies and our flashlight and set
off in the direction of the lights, about a mile away.
Midway in our walk, we distinguished the faint sound of
singing through the jungle breeze. I tilted my head this
way and that to catch the sounds. Dennis recognized the
beautiful music as a Spanish hymn.

With the music of human voices to guide us, we
walked the remaining distance along the cragged trail
without speaking. I entertained the notion that we were
like pilgrims being drawn to worship at a journey's end.
Perhaps we were.

The church music that accompanied our passage
through the dark produced a profound sereneness in me.
I had been wrestling with my guilt over not trusting God
since our landing. The experience of now hearing this
sweet music and feeling a mixture of relief and fatigue
was so poignant I was nearly moved to tears.

Passing from the darkness of the jungle toward the
growing light in the village was strikingly symbolic to
me as I considered the events of the day. I wondered to
what extent God had been involved in allowing all
of this to happen. No matter: The message of his
providence and ability to deliver had gotten through to

me. *It's a good thing his patience isn't tried by our impatience,* I thought.

Nearing the small wooden church from which the simple a capella singing appeared to be coming, we concluded the music was part of a New Year's Eve observance. About fifty people, dressed for the most part in simple white linen clothing, were assembled in the building.

We startled the congregation as we walked through the door and quietly took places in the last row. Rows of heads turned to look until the whole assembly was gazing at us in amazement.

Dennis grinned broadly, acknowledging each glance. I nodded and simply continued trying to sing the Spanish words in the tattered hymnal in my hands.

At the conclusion of the hymn, the church's minister left his place in the front of the worshippers and walked down the aisle toward us. He took our hands and smiled graciously, all the while showing puzzlement over the appearance of these two mysterious American visitors.

Dennis quickly spoke several words in Spanish, returning the minister's greetings. In a moment, the entire congregation of the Magdalena church was crowded around us.

Happily assuming the role of spokesman, Dennis began to relate the details of our ordeal. As he spoke, I observed a peculiar transformation in him—one I had seen before when he was in the company of South American Indians.

None of the shyness he usually exhibited in the company of his peers on base was evident. He was animated and talkative, with a wonderful glow of exuberance on his face. His audience listened attentively as he recounted our adventure for them in Spanish. His talent as a storyteller produced ripples of laughter among the sea of bronze faces one minute and sad shakes of the head the next.

It was almost as if a switch had been thrown somewhere in my partner's brain. I grew amused at Dennis's uncharacteristic appetite for human interaction, and pondered the reasons for this change. Why would a person who is usually so shy around the people with whom he works and lives suddenly become so comfortable and good-natured around these Indians?

The Indians certainly acted as if we were walking confirmations of God's love and guidance. Our appearance had been nothing short of dramatic. Perhaps Dennis felt this, too. I concluded it was his strong sense of compassion for these extremely impoverished people that produced his unusual demonstration of warmth and openness.

Shifting my attention to the tribespeople flocked around us, I was tremendously gratified to see their radiant faces and broad smiles as they rejoiced with us over our deliverance. When Dennis finished speaking, there was backslapping all around and sincere offerings of praise to God by these Spanish-speaking Christians.

It was certainly fulfilling for me to experience this open fellowship with these strangers, who, having put aside any cultural barriers that might normally exist, felt genuinely uplifted by the unexpected visit of two lost missionaries.

As overcome as I was by this display of Christian love, I also felt the pangs of hunger and fatigue. I was anticipating an offer of food and a place to sleep for the night at any moment.

My Spanish was adequate in most places, but I understood little of the rapid conversation that evolved between Dennis and our new Indian friends. After another round of smiles and backslapping, Dennis turned to me giddily.

"They want us to sing a duet as an expression of thanksgiving for our deliverance," he said with a grin. "It's their custom."

"You mean they want us to sing?" I asked, trying not to look too perplexed in front of our smiling hosts.

"Yeah," he said, laughing. "We gotta do it. I'll find something easy in the hymnbook."

I was frankly surprised that we should be called upon to sing after having undergone such an emotionally draining ordeal only minutes before. I relented graciously. I felt some security in knowing that Dennis had a pretty good voice and enough fluency in Spanish to pull off the duet.

Dennis was obviously delighted to honor the request of these people with whom he felt such a strong attachment, and he eagerly took the small stage.

Here I go, relying on Dennis again, I thought as I gamely followed him to the stage. *Imagine, making my singing debut miles and miles deep in the heart of the Amazonian jungle.*

Dennis selected a simple Spanish hymn with few verses. A guitarist had appeared at the corner of the stage to accompany us. My partner sang out with gusto, to the enjoyment of our small Amazonian audience. I sang the best I could in unison with him, not at all annoyed by the fact that his robust vocalization drowned out my voice completely.

After singing for our supper, as it were, the two of us were fed the Amazonian staples of papaya, mango, bread, and beef. The minister put us up for the night in his hut. Inside, we found two wooden cots with thin mattresses. They looked wonderful.

Before lying down to sleep, I knelt beside my cot on the hard earthen floor of the primitive hut. With tears streaming down my face, I thanked God for bringing Dennis and me through our perilous incident in the plane.

I thanked him that I would see my family again, and that my future—which had seemed in such great doubt earlier—was once again in place. And I thanked him that he could be so patient with my impatience.

I awoke around dawn to see the first rays of morning light streaming through our window. Dennis had rounded up a small ration of gasoline that would carry us the remaining part of our journey home. After saying our good-byes to the San José villagers, we gathered our belongings and headed out on the mile-long walk to our plane. We were quickly airborne, cruising far above the awakening jungle world below as a dazzling sunrise heralded the beginning of a new day and a new year.

➡️ *He that dwelleth in the secret place of the most High shall abide under the shadow of the Almighty* (Ps. 91:1, KJV).

➡️ *Weeping may endure for a night, but joy cometh in the morning* (Ps. 30:5, KJV).

➡️ *None can believe how powerful prayer is, and what it is able to effect, but those who have learned it by experience* (Martin Luther).

CHAPTER

THE GREAT FAMILY
SAILING DISASTER

I was already wide-eyed when my watch emitted its little
electronic chirp, telling me it was 5:30. What sounded
like hungry seagulls fighting over a morning meal
outside our Destin, Florida, motel room had roused me
from a half-sleep several minutes earlier.

When the alarm had gone off, I was staring into the
darkness, trying to sort out the thoughts that had jutted
into my dreams during the past few hours. In my mind, I
was alternating between two different issues—some
complicated business matters involving my psychiatric
practice in Chattanooga, Tennessee, and the challenging
sailing trip that lay before me and my untried, but
enthusiastic crew.

Now that I was wide awake, however, I could shake
off my somber, disjointed thoughts of business legal
proceedings and entertain more pleasing images: ropes

pulled taut and knotted, white sails puffed with the wind, and a sleek, angular hull rippling through glassy waters.

This, I vowed with all the zest I could muster, *is going to be a great day . . . if it kills me.*

With a little hop, I vigorously threw my legs over the edge of my bed and sat up. My eagerness to begin the first leg of our family's long-awaited sea-faring journey made it seem like Christmas Day had come in the middle of July—or so I had tried to convince myself.

Our family had enlarged to include two sons, who would be expected to play large roles in our sailing excursion. David, fourteen, had been born prior to our year's stint in South America. Dale, our youngest, had entered the world in Gainesville, Florida, during my psychiatric training and had just turned ten. Carey, now twenty-one, had been included in our sailing plans at the last minute along with her fiancé, Chris, also twenty-one. They'd met at Baylor University.

As for the skipper, I had earnestly pursued my dreams of becoming a psychiatrist. My additional years of training and subsequent private practice in Chattanooga had opened up opportunities to speak and write on my special interests in child-rearing and family counseling.

I debated momentarily whether to awaken Pat and Carey, who were sleeping in the other bed in the room, but decided instead to let them catch a few extra winks; they would need their strength.

As for our two sons, David and Dale, and Carey's fiancé Chris, all of whom were sharing the adjoining suite, I presumed they were still snoring. David and Dale would be, anyway. I knew they enjoyed their sleep too much to let a few noisy gulls crack the cocoons of their slumber.

After fumbling in the dark for my clothes, I dressed quickly, finally donning my captain's cap with the snappy cheerfulness of a kid. I stepped out onto our gulf-front balcony and into a quiescent coastal world that shortly would begin stretching to life. Only the activity of the rambunctious water birds and early-rising workers at a nearby pier disturbed the otherwise dormant Florida gulf setting.

I took in a deep draft of the slightly muggy, salt-swept morning air and leaned against the railing. The sun was just beginning to rise; its flaming upper ridge shot pink trails into the sky and across the placid waters stretched in front of me.

I was determined not to let this spectacular sunrise get away before sharing it with my best first mate, but I felt moved first to use this moment of solitude to reflect on God's goodness. I was grateful he had provided the opportunity for this family outing, one which represented for me the realization of a lifelong dream.

I must have been about fifteen when I was assigned to read segments of Melville's *Moby Dick* and began to fancy myself as a salty character on the high seas. Although the teacher's explanations of symbols, metaphors, and such put me off slightly, my yearning for rugged ocean adventure like the *Pequod's* crew had undergone remained strong.

There's little doubt that this romantic vision of coursing the seas led me to choose a career in the navy. However, when I applied for admission to the U.S. Naval Academy in Annapolis at the age of eighteen, my most dominant motive was not lust for adventure, but relief of college education costs for my parents. A national grocery store chain had intruded into Albuquerque and forced my father to close his neighborhood grocery store business.

Concluding my prayers with thanks for a family of my own that was loving enough to go along with dear old dad's dream, I reentered the room to awaken Pat.

With the dawn's pale light beginning to slip its way into our room, I bent over and put my mouth close to Pat's ear. Playfully, I lightly whistled the four-toned boatswain's signal for attention.

"All hands on deck," I whispered.

Pat rolled over and smiled sleepily.

"Aye, aye, captain."

She joined me shortly on the balcony. A sleepy smile broke across her face when she saw the gulf sunrise now blazing in full glory.

"It's gorgeous," she said, sighing. "You want to wake up the kids and go get some breakfast?"

"Yeah. I'm ready to go."

We were served breakfast in the motel's rotating tower restaurant. The food was good, but the panoramic view of the sun-bleached shores and soft-breaking waters of the Florida gulf was magnificent. Afterwards, we piled into our car and headed out to charter our sloop.

The mood among us was absolutely buoyant as we traveled the brief coastal stretch to the boat rental marina. Indeed, our trip thus far had been as idyllic and as satisfying as we had hoped. The ten-hour drive from our Signal Mountain, Tennessee, home had seemed much shorter, being filled with giddy talk about our grand, five-day gulf cruise.

I couldn't resist predicting, "You kids are in for the time of your lives," as we pulled into the marina's parking lot.

Confidently, I strode up to the dilapidated, gray-wooded shack that bore a sign reading "boat rentals." Once inside, I marched up to the counter and informed several grizzled old attendants, who were talking and reading the paper, that the Campbell family was here to get its sailboat.

I was sorry to see the men were slightly annoyed. I mean, after all, I wasn't just another tourist, but a former naval officer. We weren't going half-cocked into this thing. One of the men stood up and looked me over. I was glad I'd left my captain's cap in the car. I only wished my white pants and Keds sneakers weren't quite so clean and white.

"We gotta put ya through the paces, first," he spoke

smugly through tobacco-stained lips. "Y'all qualified to bareboat?"

Bareboating is the term used to describe sailing without the assistance of a professional crew. I told him that all of us, except Carey and Chris, had taken the basic sailing courses offered by the Annapolis Sailing School the previous summer, and that Pat and myself were graduates of advanced bareboating courses. For good measure, I added that Carey had taught some sailing classes at summer camp once. I leaned one arm on the counter, satisfied that I had impressed this salt-cured geezer.

The unshaven character twisted up his mouth as he sized up the group, now standing with me around the counter. My crew wasn't big and strong, but it was intelligent and wiry.

David, Dale, and Chris represented the brawn of my crew, despite the fact that neither David nor Chris weighed one hundred and fifty pounds soaking wet. Pat and Carey were the brains and heart of the group. Rather than give the marina staff any more cause to resent us by ticking off the characteristics I admired in each individual, we waited patiently for the manager to give further instructions.

Bareboating is big business, especially in the Florida gulf, where the water is a great deal more smooth than on the open coasts. Boats like the oceangoing, thirty-foot Erickson sloop we were signing up for were expensive vessels, so I understood the requirement of showing the boat rental people my qualifications in sailing. I was poised, however, to inform the old gentleman that he was talking to an Annapolis graduate, not some yahoo who wanted to take the family out on a lark. I hoped he wouldn't let it get that far.

Abruptly, the old fellow put down the pen he'd been fiddling with and walked around the counter to the front door of the shack.

"Awwright," he hollered toward the docks. "Gimme number twelve."

He spit in the sand outside before returning behind the counter.

"OK, folks," he said, his smile revealing an uneven row of brownish teeth. "Let's get you signed up and take you out for your big test."

Shortly we were all out in the bay with a younger, considerably more pleasant attendant. It soon became obvious that the only one really being tested was me, the captain. But the crew had to perform some skills, too. We did well in coming about and jibing. The man-overboard drills were a little more difficult for us, because the Erickson sloop handled differently from the sailboats we had trained on, and Chris, Carey, and Dale were just plain inexperienced.

Finally, they determined we were competent.

After the go-ahead from the boat rental people, we loaded up our belongings and a five-day ration of groceries and climbed back on board to make our preparations to get underway.

We'd decided beforehand that rather than head immediately into the Intercoastal Waterway, we would anchor a short way out in Destin Bay and spend the day gaining our bearings. Being the captain, I naturally felt compelled to familiarize my crew with the fine points of proper sailing. It didn't occur to me until I'd wasted several hours of breath that the only rule the crew had in mind was to have fun.

"Oh well," I said, finally relenting. "We've got plenty of time to get down to the serious business of sailing." I did manage to squeeze some instruction in between the snorkeling and sunbathing.

Before long, after the crew had sufficiently frolicked in the hot, hot sun, the question of where to sleep came up.

I was a little taken aback. "Aren't we going to sleep

onboard out here?" I lightly punched the air with my fist. "We're roughin' it, aren't we?"

A chorus of "Awws" came back. "I think we ought to find a nice marina, where we can get something to eat and freshen up a little," Pat suggested.

"OK, I'm no Captain Bligh," I joked. "You win." I was eager to get in some sailing anyway.

Following the coastal traffic, we made our way after about an hour into the Blue Water Bay Marina. The marina was right out of a storybook; it reminded the kids of scenes from the television program "Fantasy Island," with its waterfalls and luxuriant tropical plant life. A great meal in the marina restaurant was the perfect end to a perfect day.

An unexpected shuffle ensued as we prepared to bed down on board for the night. David, Carey, and Chris gave up trying to get situated in their respective bunks, and grabbed their pillows and sheets to sleep on the dock.

Pat tranquilized my protests with a gentle shaking of her head. "They're OK," she said. I knew the quarters were a little uncomfortable due to the cramped, sultry conditions, but they had to understand this was not a fine cabin cruiser.

I shrugged it off and rolled over to sleep. "They'll get in the swing of things tomorrow."

At exactly 5:30, my wristwatch beeped its alarm. Pat was already awake. My eyes found hers in the darkness.

"Hot night, huh?" she whispered.

"Yeah, I guess the one thing we didn't plan for was the heat. We could use an air conditioner. I'll rig a wind tunnel tomorrow night."

The night before, Pat had offered to get up early with me, permitting the others to sleep later. She and I would head the boat out into the gulf's Intercoastal Waterway toward our destination at Pensacola Bay. We wanted to start early enough to avoid sailing at night.

Once on deck, I could see from the circles under her eyes she'd gotten little sleep. "You ready to go?" I asked.

"Whenever you are," she replied. "Let me get the kids back onboard."

The first fishing boats had only just left their slips in the marina, and the wakes created by their passage caused our sloop to rock and bump slightly against the dock. I could scarcely wait to join them.

First, I joined our mainsail to the mast and boom. Then I attached the main halyard to the mainsail so the heavy canvas sheet would be ready to hoist after we cleared the channel.

From the dock I flipped the lines onboard. My hurried, excited movements nearly caused me to lose my step and fall back into the boat. *Glad my crew didn't see that,* I thought. Once safely in, I started our diesel inboard motor with the turn of a key, and shoved hard with both hands to clear the dock.

Creeping along at a speed of several knots, we made our way out of the marina's small channel into Choctawhatchee Bay. Pretty soon we had reached the point where we could cut our engine and hoist our mainsail and unfurl the jib. The winds were light, but surprisingly brisk for this early in the morning.

With Pat's help the sail was hoisted; it billowed gracefully as I trimmed the sails for a port tack position with the wind. It was nearly seven o'clock when we moved into the heart of the bay. The sun, just off our starboard side, felt good on our faces and arms.

By eight o'clock, the sun had risen measurably above the horizon, and already we could sense the day was going to be a hot one. But cutting along in the sparkling gulf waters, with a good coastal breeze and an occasional ocean spray blowing defiantly in your face, who could complain?

Shortly, I learned who, as the peanut gallery began

stirring to life in the cabin in front of me.

"Gaaah-lee, it's gettin' hot!" David blurted out in disgust. "I'm gonna take a shower."

Stubbornly, I fought to disregard David's negative comments and remain unfazed—as captains should. But the continued grumbling about the heat began to get to me. Admittedly, we, or I should say I, had not prepared for the heat, which was beginning to grow intense on this first leg of our trip to Pensacola.

Sloops even smaller than the one we had chartered could be equipped with air-conditioning. In my excitement, however, I hadn't even inquired about a wind funnel to facilitate ventilation. Nor had I checked the weather forecasts that were calling for blistering, above normal temperatures. Fighting my feelings of disgust, I doubted that my plans to use a sheet as a wind funnel would be adequate.

Pat brought me out of my thoughts by resting her arm on my shoulder.

"How long should it take us to get to Fort Walton?" she asked.

It was about nine o'clock. Judging from the map, the narrow channel of Fort Walton was probably another half hour away.

"About thirty minutes," I informed her. "Got anything to drink?"

She returned several moments later with two glasses of chilled orange juice. The cold liquid tasted good going down. I could hear David and Dale tussling in the cabin behind me. I was eager to share all of this wide-open beauty with them.

I cocked my cap back on my head with my glass to catch some of the breeze on my sweating forehead.

"Heat or no heat, this is the life," I said to myself.

"Mom!" Dale suddenly called out in exasperation. "Don't we have an air conditioner on this thing?"

Almost as I had predicted, within thirty minutes we were approaching the narrow channel of Fort Walton. Now my seamanship would be put to the test. Passing through the channel, which is almost a narrow river, would be especially difficult, as there happened to be a lot of intercoastal traffic, including several tugboats and barges.

I was closely surveying the movements of the vessels to my right when I suddenly detected a wisp of smoke to my left. Then I smelled it. I turned quickly to see black smoke wafting from one side of the cabin hatch. I expected the words I heard next.

"Oh my gosh!" Carey screamed. "There's a fire in here!"

"Fire! Someone help me!" Chris yelled out.

With a rag he was beating back sheets of flames spewing from beneath and behind our alcohol stove just inside the cabin's aft hatch.

I began to run in the direction of the cabin. "Help!" Chris screamed again.

By this time, Carey, David, and Dale had scampered out of the fore hatch of the cabin. Alcohol had somehow leaked out from the stove onto the wooden deck. The fire spread out like a tumbling wave. Flames and smoke were boiling furiously out of the cabin's aft hatch. I was absolutely terrified.

Pat and Carey circled around behind me, completely panicked, as I struggled against the licking flames and thick black smoke to unfasten the two fire extinguishers on the bulkhead beside the cabin steps.

I heaved one of the extinguishers to Chris, who failed to see it coming through the smoke. It hit the deck with a thud. In a moment, he was emitting large blasts of white powder from the extinguisher in the direction of the smoke-shrouded stove.

I glanced over my shoulder to view our sloop's progress as I loosened the pin on my fire extinguisher. Apparently, someone aboard the barge nearest us had

noticed our perilous situation, because the tugs had
begun slowing the mammoth steel vessel to a stop. We
didn't pose a threat to any of them yet. Our most
immediate concern was that our boat, now making
erratic movements in the narrow channel, would run
aground.

I sent one long blast from the extinguisher in the
direction of the blaze as I made my way down into the
cabin. Standing in opposite sides of the small
compartment, Chris and I worked the extinguishers'
black nozzles to and fro into the smoke and fire, pouring
forth wide streams of the thick white chemical. Within
several minutes, the fire had been put out.

Immediately, Chris and I dashed to the fore cabin
hatch and lunged upward through it. We entered the
opening at the same instant, knocking our heads together
in Three Stooges-fashion as we coughed and gasped for
breath.

In the meantime, Carey was struggling single-handedly
to untie the small rubber emergency dinghy alongside
the cabin.

"Help me, Mom!" she was shouting frantically. "Hurry!
We're going to burn up if we don't get out of here!"

David had thrown our only bucket overboard to
retrieve some water to help put out the fire.
Unfortunately, in doing so he had failed to grab hold of
the line attached to the handle. He and Dale helplessly
watched as the tin container sank.

"The fire's out!" I bellowed. "It's out!"

Carey and Pat dropped the dinghy. Everyone scurried
over to the cabin's rear opening to inspect the damage.
As the smoke and powder began to clear, we were
flabbergasted by what we saw. On everything, it
seemed—the walls, the bunks, the deck, the ceiling, the
table and, of course, the stove—there was a good two
inches of the white extinguisher chemical. It looked like
a major snowstorm had erupted in the cabin. Judging

from the relative ease with which the fire had been brought under control, our firefighting efforts represented a case of massive overkill.

Had I not been so startled initially by the blaze, it would have dawned on me that alcohol burns at a very low temperature, which is why alcohol stoves are chosen for use on sailing vessels like ours. The fire warranted none of the extreme measures we took; in fact, if we had left it alone, it probably would have gone out by itself.

The realization that I had been a party to all the panic despite knowing better, coupled with the sight of our powder-coated cabin, produced a surge of anger in me.

I threw the empty extinguisher against the surrounding cabinets near the helm in a fit of outrage. Grabbing the helm, I pulled us out of a spin and redirected our course before we ran aground. When the sloop was under control, I turned on my stunned family.

"Do you all realize we're going to have to pay for this mess?" I roared. "I can't believe the utter stupidity here. What happened, Chris? What in the world did you do? How could you be so negligent?"

I looked over at Carey's fiancé. I was far too upset to see anything humorous about his appearance, although later we all laughed heartily at the sight of the two of us. He looked like a victim of a flour factory explosion. A sickened look covered his smudged, perspiring face. His arms hung limply at his side. I'm sure I looked equally as bad.

Chris looked me directly in the face.

"I'm sorry," he said defensively, obviously hurt by my abusive statements.

"He was trying to make some coffee, Dad," Carey explained indignantly. "He didn't know how to light the stove."

True to my inclination to throw in the towel after a disappointment, I suggested that we just forget the whole thing and return the boat, since we had not yet reached the halfway point of our trip.

As usual, Pat came to the rescue, saving the day for everyone. She calmed me down and told me no real harm had been done. She and Carey and the boys would "clean things up" while I battled the waterway traffic.

David protested. "What do I have to clean up this mess for? I didn't do it. We don't even have a vacuum cleaner!"

Pat focused her blue eyes at David in an icy glare that could have chased the freckles right off his face.

"Come on," she said, grabbing him by the shoulder and guiding him down the cabin steps into the chemical glaze.

Joining the others in the task of cleaning up, fun-loving Dale tried to slide his feet across the cabin deck.

"Hey, it's snow!" he called out in delight. "It's Christmas!"

Indeed, at daybreak it had seemed like Christmas in July—even before our cabin had been flocked to resemble a winter wonderland. I had awoken with the anticipation of finally living out my fantasy. Now, my mood had turned to resentment and agitation—like that of an old Scrooge. The childlike, blithe spirit with which I had begun the day was gone. In my present state I felt a little silly wearing my captain's cap, so I tossed it on the cushioned seats behind me.

With our sloop only twenty or thirty yards from the most narrow point in the channel, I could not fall back and brood. After several vigorous tugs at the helm, I brought our sailboat in a proper line to proceed through the channel. Then I turned on the ship's auxiliary engine and debated how best to bring in the sails without ruffling any more feathers.

Chris was leaning against the cabin's outer bulkhead, his eyes fixed blankly in the direction we were headed. He was obviously feeling a little awkward at this point and was taking some time to try and collect himself. I felt a surge of guilt building within me.

By now I had cooled down somewhat, despite the scorching late morning sun that mercilessly beat down upon us. Recalling how I had unloaded my ire upon Chris made me wince. I could just imagine how he was thinking of his future father-in-law—this psychiatrist who made a living espousing Christian principles of tolerance, tenderness, and self-control—presuming, that is, he still thought of me as a future father-in-law.

Here was a young man who, I figured, must see himself as an outsider, an intruder on this long-awaited family outing, and before things had even reached the halfway point he finds himself responsible for a fire that threatened not only the trip itself, but the lives of everyone on board.

You blew it, I thought to myself. *You really blew it. This poor guy's doing his best to impress the Campbell family, and you're tearing into him as if he were some stranger off the street.*

The real truth of the matter was that I had been negligent in not showing Chris and the others how to operate the stove. Chris had apparently turned the fuel knob on and left it there, as one does with a gas stove. Alcohol stoves, however, require only a small amount of alcohol fumes to light them.

I struggled with how I might open positive communication between Chris and myself. I didn't have to fabricate an opportunity: I desperately needed his help in bringing in our sails before we entered the heart of the channel. It seemed as good a way as any to try and smooth things over with him.

I called over to him in the friendliest voice I could manage.

"Uh, Chris. Could I get you to help me pull in our mainsail?"

"Yeah, sure," he responded politely.

I knew an apology was in order. I'm sure he did, too. But I couldn't bring myself to it. It was as if a knot right in the center of my diaphram prevented me from verbalizing my feelings of remorse to him. I grappled with this inner conflict for several moments. At last I succumbed to thinking that the tension would dissolve by itself.

Bringing up the incident would only make things more awkward, I thought to myself as we strained with the lines to pull down the heavy canvas sails.

"It's gettin' hot, isn't it?" I said lamely.

"Yeah, it sure is," was his reply.

Having helped complete the task of lashing the mainsail to the boom, he glanced up at me. His expression gave away his feelings of self-consciousness.

"I'm going to go see if Carey and Mrs. Campbell need any help," he said.

Through the aft hatch I could see Pat and Carey on their hands and knees mopping up the white residue with towels.

Our sailboat, now puttering along at a mere three or four knots, was dwarfed in the busy channel by the huge barges and other commercial vessels. My ill feelings were beginning to melt away, and I was getting back into the fun of things—going under bridges and maneuvering our passage among the barges. I was glad now that I had realized Pat's wisdom in putting the pieces together after the fire and carrying on. I really didn't want to ruin the entire trip by going back. High adventure. That's what I wanted.

So why did I suggest going back? I'd caught myself using this tactic before when I wanted to ventilate anger after some planned family event had gone awry. My motive, usually, was to force them to share in my unhappiness. But this time the intensity of my tantrum surprised even me.

"As soon as we get past Fort Walton and the channel spreads out, we can really begin to sail," I called out optimistically, hoping to bolster our spirits. Sensing the heat building up on my head, I reached for my cap and slapped it in place.

By now the chore of cleaning up the cabin had been completed, and Pat joined me at the helm. She looked spent. It had taken Chris and myself a scant five minutes or so to empty the extinguisher tanks, but it took Pat and the others nearly three hours to wipe up the mess. A gooey paste, created from her perspiration and the chemical material, clung to her arms and legs. Her face was red, and her clothes were practically wringing wet.

She blew out a sigh of exasperation as she looked at me.

"Want some lunch?" she asked with a weak smile.

"Yeah. That'd be great," I responded, trying to sound upbeat and encouraging. "What's the cabin look like?"

"Oh, it's pretty clean," she answered. "We can't get the powder out of the cracks in the floor, though."

"The deck," I corrected playfully.

"Yeah, the deck."

We were through the channel when Pat reappeared with some sandwiches and ice water. I expected a stiff gulf wind momentarily to reach out to us over the widening waters and send us clipping on our merry way to Pensacola, but, to my chagrin, what little wind had been present in the channel had dissipated totally. An unrelenting sun was edging the mercury in our rusted thermometer up near one hundred degrees. I truly believed we could have fried an egg on the fiberglass deck.

Everyone had stripped down to their bathing suits except me—I continued to wear my knit shirt and cotton trousers. I had kicked off my sneakers, though. The kids were trying to stay cool by rubbing themselves with ice and wetted cloths. Their efforts, however, produced little relief.

I guess it was at this point that the different expectations about the trip became apparent. On my vacations, I love to throw myself into exciting adventures—as long as they're not too dangerous or uncomfortable, of course. And I was bound to have my exciting adventure here. I had just assumed that everyone else was along for the same reason.

"I mean, what are a few inconveniences when we're having a wonderful, exciting adventure?" That was my attitude, and I couldn't understand why no one else shared it.

Not only did none of the kids share this attitude, but, to my dismay, they held it in great contempt. Sure it was hot. Hot was an inconvenience. But we had to take the good with the bad.

The younger, pampered (if I may be so bold) generation begged to differ, however. And on this trip, its spokesman was David.

"Can we stop and go swimmin'?" he moaned from the bow. "We're roastin'!"

Anchoring so close to the channel at Fort Walton was out of the question due to the heavy traffic. I also felt we couldn't afford to curtail what little progress we were making, with Pensacola still a long way away. Pat and I had decided to try to dock at a marina at Pensacola, where we could all freshen up and have a good meal. What's more, if we broke for a period of recreation, we'd force ourselves to sail further into the evening, weakening our chances to find a vacant slip for the night.

"David, we have to keep moving," Pat explained. "We need to be in Pensacola before dark. The wind will pick up shortly and we can begin sailing again."

Her manner, as usual, was calm and reassuring. But David, who I kiddingly describe as having been born giving the doctor instructions, was of another mind.

"You don't know that!" he snapped loudly. "We're gonna fry out here! We're not even movin', hardly! This is really the pits! We ought to be swimming and having fun! I never want to do this again!"

"OK, David, you've said your piece," I shot back, perturbed. I realized he was probably voicing the sentiments of the entire group. For all I knew, Pat's attitude was no different from his. As for me, I was still clinging to my determination to have fun at this bareboating foolishness. But even I, too, was beginning to grow weary from the heat and stress.

David sat down in a huff on the bow and redraped the wet towel over his head and shoulders.

I bit my lip to keep from saying anything more. Needless to say, our first full day of sailing could not have gone any worse. Devastating heat, no wind, and a speed of five knots was not high adventure. For some people, the fire we had on board would be the highest kind of adventure. Even I draw the line somewhere.

Our stress and discomfort rose with the midday sun. Until now there had been enough adventure to keep me happy, but David's harsh remarks about never wanting to go sailing again kept echoing in my ears. There was no question that choosing the middle of July to sail the Intercoastal Waterway on the northwest Florida coast had been a mistake.

Certainly, the heat wouldn't have been so bad if we'd been on a power boat, which can go anywhere from twenty-five to fifty miles an hour. But this was a seagoing sailboat. They don't expect you to need a motor when you can sail. Nor an air conditioner, I guess, when you can swim or fan yourself. I pictured the crusty boat rental manager laughing at us from afar.

I pulled off my cap and ran my hand through my wet hair. The cap slipped from my hand and fell onto the deck. I didn't bother to pick it up, but pushed it out of the way with my foot.

The steady drone of the tiny diesel engine had become a source of annoyance for me. I repeatedly looked up at the sloop's sail-barren mast, not knowing exactly what I expected to see. Without a sail, the mast, resembling a huge, polished cross, was worthless to us.

Even the beautiful, sun-dazzled waters, which had been so appealing at the outset of the day's sailing, had taken on a mundane, blue-gray sameness. No longer did the spray from our wake produce the appearance of so many diamonds being churned up; there was now virtually no wake at all. The kids, still sprawled around the bow with damp towels over their heads and shoulders to shield the sun, resembled a group of sunbathing sheiks. David, bored and sunburned, dangled his hand over the side, occasionally stretching his arm to play with the small wake or rewetting his towel by slapping it into the sea.

My eyes had begun to hurt from the sun's brilliant reflection off the white fiberglass bulkheads. My exposed neck and arms felt tender and my legs ached from my extended post at the wheel. The stifling humidity had made breathing difficult hours ago.

Nagged by the fear that another disaster would materialize at the hands of my inexperienced crew, I prayed for deliverance in the form of wind. I would have been content with several inches of snow. Deep drifts of it. As it was, we were nearly out of ice, having used far more than we had expected. I glanced at my watch; I was surprised to see it was almost six o'clock.

Within an hour, as we neared Pensacola Bay, the wind suddenly picked up, so much so that the waters grew choppy. I didn't waste any time giving orders to attach and hoist the sails. I was amazed at how quickly the glassy smooth sea had been transformed. I didn't put too much stock in the notion that I had influenced this sudden change in conditions with my prayers, but I wasn't going to sell the Lord short, either. I pictured him stretching his hand over the waterway, as he did over the Sea of Galilee, and saying, "They've suffered enough."

By this time everyone was thoroughly drained. Because the winds were blowing against us when we got to Pensacola Bay, we were forced to tack, that is, to approach the wind from the left and then the right at a forty-five degree angle.

Very early in the trip, I had figured we would simply

rough it and anchor out every night. But from the forlorn looks on the sunburned faces of my crew, I knew that such a suggestion would be an invitation to mutiny.

I turned to Pat for some input on how best to keep our disenchanted crew from growing any testier during our stopover in Pensacola Bay. She was seated on one of the cushions that form the lounging area around the helm, applying generous amounts of aloe lotion to her reddened legs.

"I am simply burned up," she groaned. "I knew it would happen."

I reminisced about the night we had met on a blind date in her hometown of Pensacola. She sat silently as I reminded her of how she and her girlfriend had showed up painfully sunburned, having fallen asleep in the sun earlier that day.

"You two were as red as painted lobsters," I laughed. "Remember?" She didn't seem amused by the recollection.

"Well, anyway," I said, returning to the subject of where to dock, "What shall we do about tonight?"

"How about the yacht club in Pensacola?" she suggested. "The kids'll love it there."

I was thrilled with her excellent idea. I'd forgotten the recommendation of a friend of ours in Chattanooga, who frequently sails the Intercoastal Waterway route.

"Great. Now that's the Ritz, but it'll be worth it. We'll get in and clean up a little bit, and everyone will feel a lot better after a good meal. Maybe we can do some fishing."

I was committed to salvaging something out of this day.

Shortly we were entering the long river inlet that leads to the lagoon of the Pensacola Yacht Club.

Now our sloop looked fine to us, but a thirty-foot sailboat is just not the luxurious upper yacht club type like the one our wealthy friend owned. But we decided to barge right into the club anyway. We glided toward the docks, helped by a slight breeze in the inlet, and made a nice landing just as the sun was beginning its descent behind the surrounding thicket of pine and palm trees. At least we looked seaworthy.

After docking, I delegated the task of tying up the boat to Carey and Chris. David, Dale, Pat, and myself busied ourselves with securing the sails and stowing the loose gear on board.

As we disembarked, I nearly fell over the morass of rope woven in a cobweb-like fashion between the boat and several pylons alongside the dock. My anger boiled up from out of nowhere.

"What in the world is all of this?" I complained loudly. "This won't do. It just won't do. I should have done it myself!"

Chris and Carey stepped back, completely surprised by the verbal barrage directed at them. The others stood motionless, equally stunned.

"Just get out of the way," I yelled. "Everybody just go on up to the office and wait for me."

After some time spent untying and retying the heavy lengths of rope, a sickening awareness grew in me— Carey and Chris had been right all along; their methods in tying the knots were unorthodox, but at least they had allowed a spring line that prevented the boat from rubbing against the huge wooden pylons. Swallowing my pride, I retied the lines in the original manner.

I felt like a dam was ready to break inside me. I wasn't so sure it hadn't already begun. My extreme agitation prevented me from thinking clearly. As I trudged up the small hill toward the club office, I kept asking myself, *What's the matter with me?*

After a cool shower and a change of clothes, my mood had improved considerably. I hoped the refreshing pause from the travails of sailing the Florida gulf in July had similarly lifted the spirits of everyone else.

I thought, *Surely all of this will put everybody in a great mood.*

That hope never materialized. Through the remainder of the night, even during dinner, Carey and Chris conversed only between themselves. When I was able (or intentionally permitted) to listen in on their rather solemn chatter, they agonized over the painfulness of their sunburn and the reality of spending *three more days* in this unbearable heat.

All of us kept avoiding the disapproving glances of the restaurant's management, who looked as if it was going to show us to our sailboat for dragging out our meal into a three-hour marathon to enjoy the restaurant's cool confines.

After dinner, we decided to briefly try our hands at fishing before turning in. Carey and Chris balked at the idea and maintained their distance. It didn't take an authority on human behavior to see there was more to their aloofness than the desire merely to be alone. Guilt and hurt bubbled up in me once more. I wanted so much to share my passion for this sailing adventure, to make this an unforgettable event in everyone's lives. Unforgettable it would be, but for all the wrong reasons.

At bedtime, to add injury to insult, Carey, Chris, and David collected their bunk cushions, sheets, and pillows and climbed out onto the dock to sleep. I granted them the fact that it was warm in the cabin, but at least inside we didn't have to contend with the mosquitoes and moths and the harsh glare of the dock lights.

I felt I had some wounds that needed licking, but I didn't lick them long. After offering my burdens to the Lord and asking for strength (and no more fires), I lay down on my bunk, too exhausted to be annoyed by my sunburned neck and face and our sheets made sticky by perspiration, and dropped into a deep sleep.

Early the next morning I was jolted out of my slumber when the boat dipped to one side and started to rock. The motion was created by the footsteps of our three docksiders, who, judging from their groggy conversation, had fared poorly during the night. Chris complained of not having slept "at all."

Soon all of us were up, and Pat and Carey teamed up to make a hearty breakfast. During our meal, everyone's sunburn and general discomfort was the dominant topic of conversation. We decided, at Pat's suggestion, to spend the day touring the historic district in Pensacola. The pause, Pat pointed out, would provide ample shade and air-conditioning to give our tender hides a welcome reprieve.

The historic district of restored buildings was simply beautiful, and our seafood lunch in Pensacola could not have been any better. In an effort to keep everybody happy, we had taken a cab nearly everywhere we went. But as I studied the faces of the kids every now and again, I could tell they were still bored and unhappy.

"Well, now what do I do?" I said, turning to Pat. "I'm doing everything I can. And I'm spending much more than I had anticipated, docking at the marinas and riding around Pensacola. It's hard to believe we're even on a sailboating trip. I give up on this bunch."

"Just relax," Pat said.

"I'm doing my best."

After spending our third night on the boat, we awoke to brisk winds and a brilliant blue, virtually cloudless sky. It was time for us to make our way back across Pensacola Bay to a marina right next to a gorgeous little stretch of beach called Santa Rosa Island. Setting my sights there, we shoved off.

With a gulf stream at our backs, we sailed with ease across Pensacola Bay. At the helm, I was drinking in the tropical splendor and relishing every exhilarating moment of our best day yet. In another four hours or so we'd be at the island. Just in time for a late lunch.

Pat shared in my intoxicated mood, as did Dale and David, but Carey and Chris still looked as if they'd rather be a thousand miles away. I was sorry they felt as if I had put a crimp in their style with my overbearing zeal for sailing and my harsh commands that were barked out of necessity—and tension—and certainly not meant personally. I smiled to see Santa Rosa Island growing larger before us with each passing minute.

They'll love this. This is just the greatest place in the world, I thought.

Frolicking and lounging in the sun would be a sure tonic for anything that ails any of us, I was certain. Anything, that is, except sunburn. Pat and I had managed to keep ourselves protected with sunscreen and light clothing, and the boys were as tough-hided as gators, but Carey and Chris had simply gotten too many rays. I hurt to look at them. So the three hours or so we spent on one of the most beautiful beaches in the world were, as far as Carey and Chris were concerned, another colossal dud.

At the end of our stay on the island, we shoved off and sailed in the direction of a nearby marina where we would tie up for our final night on the boat.

Surrounded by all the sights and sounds that make the gulf one of my favorite places, we glided effortlessly through a long channel located on the south side of Pensacola Beach. The marina was just ahead.

Carey and Chris, unfortunately, were handling the lines on the bow. I shouted up at them to attach the line to the right tiller.

"Hold it tight now!" I called out.

I detected a grimace of defiance on Carey's face as she and Chris performed the chore.

As we turned to make our approach to the marina dock, the boom swung violently around, nearly hitting Dale. The line, which had been attached to the wrong tiller, was dangling limply from the free-swinging boom.

I exploded in rage.

"Grab the boom!" I hollered angrily. "Grab it! Tie off the darn thing! Carey, can't you do anything?"

Carey leapt onto the deck from the bow. There was

fire in her twenty-one-year-old eyes, the likes of which I had never seen before.

"Just back off, Dad!" she screamed. "We're doing the best we can! We aren't the sailors here, you are! Just get off our backs!"

"Yeah, Dad," David chimed in.

Chris was absolutely stunned at Carey's outpouring of emotion. I looked over at Pat. She, too, was speechless. As for me, I felt about a foot tall. I wanted to dive into the water and simply swim away.

Our boat's progress toward the marina's docks had slowed to a crawl with our sails down. We were about fifty yards from the marina, but I could feel the eyes of everyone in the channel staring at us.

"Well, I guess I'm just a pain in the neck," I said in a wounded tone. I felt hurt, angry, misunderstood, and badly shaken.

"Ross, you're not a pain in the neck," Pat said soothingly.

David let out a chuckle.

"I'm sorry," Carey said. "I'm sorry I yelled. We *are* doing the best we can."

"It's OK," Pat said. Every family needs someone like Pat to keep things in perspective.

I started the auxiliary motor. Before long, we were pulling alongside the dock.

Upon landing, I struggled, with David and Pat's help, to rig a wind funnel with a sheet in preparation for the warm night ahead. When finally we bounded onto the docks to wash up and eat dinner, I glanced back at our boat. It was none too admirable, docked there amidst all the huge, beautiful yachts, with our makeshift wind funnel flapping awkwardly in the breeze. Sunburned, tired, and disheveled, we presented a sorry sight as well.

After washing up, we had another lengthy dinner in the marina's air-conditioned restaurant and then dragged ourselves off for another hot night's sleep.

Somewhere in the wee hours of morning I awoke with a start so violent that it roused Pat.

"Are you OK?" she inquired.

"Yeah. Bad dream. It's OK, go back to sleep."

"What were you dreaming about?"

"It was nothing. Go back to sleep."

Nothing? I mused. *That was the craziest dream I think I've ever had.*

I rarely remember my dreams, but this one was etched vividly in my mind. My body cried out for rest, but I could not clear my thoughts of the powerful, bizarre elements of the dream.

For much of it, I had been rushing around our boat alone, frantically raising and lowering the sails, all the while doing my best to control the boat's course at the helm. Frequently in the dream I would stop and study the boat's ancient thermometer. The mercury would be rising and falling rapidly as if trying to keep pace with my own frenzied movements. Toward the end of my dream, I found myself bound with rope to an empty mast. Flames had sprung up around me from out of nowhere, and the sailboat had begun to sink. The dream took a final bizarre turn when I noticed it was sand, and not water, into which the boat was being swallowed.

At this point my mind had scrambled back to consciousness.

I remained prone on my bunk as I strained to interpret the peculiar, indeed, horrifying aspects of my dream. Perspiration coated my brow and trickled in tiny rivulets down the sides of my face. Even the tops of my feet were sweating.

I knew, first of all, that the dream represented an effort by my subconscious mind to sort through the calamities and disappointments of the previous days of sailing—the sudden eruption of fire, our lack of wind, the intense heat, and my short temper fueled by the mistakes of an untrained, unenthusiastic crew.

The one aspect of the dream that especially haunted

me was my solitary status on the boat. *Where was
everyone else?* I probed my tender emotions, running
over the concerns in my life as one might bother the
inflamed area around an aching tooth. It hit me at once:
My most dominant feeling in the dream was fear. And,
for all intents and purposes, I alone possessed that
feeling. I knew it stemmed primarily from the
responsibility I felt for my family's safety. It was I who
had orchestrated this seafaring trip; and it was I who best
understood the danger into which we had been thrust on
this vessel.

*But why was this fear so intense? Was it merely
the fire that had sparked my uncharacteristic
apprehension?*

A final insight crashed upon me with the force of a
mighty crescendo.

"The business at home," I muttered. "Of course!"

Indeed, I realized, the soured business dealings I was
trying to iron out with my associates had created in me a
profound sense of turmoil. All this time, I'd been
battling inwardly with what I consciously wanted to put
aside during our vacation.

At stake in the sticky business matter was not only my
reputation and professional future but, more important,
the financial foundation of my loved ones.

In my dream, I was alone on the burning, sinking
boat, being put to a martyr's death at the crosslike mast,
because the matter of the troubled business dealings lay
solely at my feet. I had not yet shared my worst fears
with Pat. The awareness of my lonely anxiety grew in
clarity as though a bank of clouds had been swept away.

Unknown to my family—and, initially, to me—I had
sought to have our little adventure on the high seas gloss
over any anxious, hesitant feelings I was experiencing.
Failing to find release from my problems through sailing,
I had grown irritable and even more fearful that trouble
was just around the bend.

My watch said 4:45. I slipped down from my bunk

and kneeled on the hard, wooden deck.

The Lord already knew what I was going through. It had been a tough year—nearly as tough, in fact, as my first year in medical school when Cathy had been born with multiple defects. Enveloped by night and my own gloom, I wept silently. My tears mingled with my perspiration and fell onto my tightly clasped hands.

How could I have gotten myself into such a mess? How could I have been so stupid and so trusting? I chided myself. I felt foolish for leaving myself unprotected against man's greed. The dam in me had finally broken.

As I wept, the word *unprotected* kept resurfacing in my thoughts. *Unprotected,* I thought. *Why didn't I have God's protection in all of this?* Ephesians 6:10, 11 came to mind: "Finally, my brethren, be strong in the Lord, and in the power of his might. Put on the whole armour of God . . ." (KJV).

I realized I didn't have God's protection—the safety of his armor—because I hadn't exercized my own will to arm myself. I had been standing naked before the wiles of my enemies and the ruler of darkness himself. I had not buckled on the belt of truth, or put on integrity as a coat of mail, or let the gospel of peace serve to steady my footing. I had not boldly taken up the sword of the Spirit or given myself wholly to prayer, as Paul had advised in such poetic language. Instead, I had relied on my own devices, my thirst for adventure, my feeble, human way of handling crises. And I had fallen flat on my face.

Many times I had put on God's armor, especially as a new Christian. It felt good to wear it when I was young and fervent in the faith. But foolishly, because of the hectic demands of life and an unwitting self-sufficiency, I had been taking it off (maybe because it was sometimes cumbersome) and letting it rust. And these were the times when I needed it most!

I'm not alone, I'm sorry to say, in casting off God's armor. I've seen far too many Christians in the middle years of their faith lose their yearning for the Spirit and choose to let their armor rust. Unfortunately, as we grow bigger physically and financially, so do our problems. There couldn't be a more crucial period in our lives to keep our armor on.

I crawled back into my bunk as quietly as I could so as not to awaken Pat. In the artificial glow cast by the dock lights, I could see she was looking right at me.

"Are you all right, Ross?" she asked.

"Yeah. I'm OK," I whispered.

"I love you," she whispered back.

"Thanks, honey. I needed that."

It had been another miserable night in the stifling cabin without air-conditioning. But at least for me the hours had produced some positive results. I felt I had a grip on my emotions and I knew what I must do. Top on the agenda was approaching Carey and Chris in a spirit of reconciliation. I threw back my sheet and made my way to the dock, where Carey, Chris, and David lay sleeping.

I awakened the three as I stumbled noisily from the sloop onto the dock.

"Dale, is that you?" David called out. "Don't try anything."

"No, it's me," I said. "I want to talk to you three."

I knelt down on one knee when I reached them. Their sleepy faces were slightly illuminated in the artificial glare of distant dock lights.

"I want to apologize for the way I've been acting," I said in a half-whisper. "I know I've been a little hard on you guys. I've got a lot on my mind with the business back home."

Carey propped herself up on one arm. "What's the matter, Dad?"

"Yeah, what's wrong?" David added.

"It's a long, drawn-out story," I replied. "But things aren't so bad that I should take everything out on you all. I've been unfair, and I'm really sorry. I want you guys to forgive me."

Carey swatted at a mosquito and looked up at me. A loving smile spread across her face.

"It's OK, Dad," she said. "I know you've been under a lot of pressure." Chris had been listening silently in the dark. He suddenly sat up.

"Yeah, Dr. Campbell. Don't worry about it," Chris said sleepily. "We haven't been very easy to get along with ourselves."

After a brief pause, David flopped back on his bedroll with a thud. "It's OK, Dad."

We awoke early the next morning to begin our journey home. By late afternoon, helped by good winds, we closed in on Destin Bay. I could see in the faces of the kids, even Pat's, the hunger for dry land and the comforts of home.

I made no pretense at hiding my own fatigue. I was more than willing to get back to the conveniences in our Signal Mountain home near Chattanooga—in particular, the air-conditioning and soft, smooth mattresses. During my naval career, I spent many more days at sea in one stretch than we had logged this past week; but I seriously doubt if even the best professional sailor could have enjoyed the conditions under which we were forced to sail.

At long last we pulled up to the chartering docks at Destin and wearily began collecting our garbage and sea-worn supplies. Emerging from the cabin with an armload of gear and trash, I looked up to see my old friend grinning his devilish grin through the same discolored teeth. He was exactly the person I expected would greet us first. His grizzled countenance, now bearing the stubble of five additional days' growth, was that of a person straining to squelch a laugh or the words, "I told you so."

I straightened up immediately and grinned back. I wasn't about to let him get the best of me.

He let a stream of tobacco juice fly into the water and reared back, his hands on his hips.

"Well, has it been hot enough fer you folks?"

"Oh, not too bad," I responded pleasantly. "We made sure we had plenty of ice. We went swimming as much as we could."

"Oh, ya did? Well, it's been plenty hot here. Near one hundred and three one day. Y'all didn't feel the heat? Looks like ya got a little too much sun."

Now I was beginning to feel the heat. I mustered every ounce of reserve I had in me.

"Naw. We love it," I said exuberantly. "My wife's from Florida and I'm from New Mexico, so we're used to it. It couldn't have been one hundred and three. It didn't feel like it with the wind blowing."

"Oh, you had good wind, huh?" he replied sarcastically. "Didn't have any other problems, did ya?"

I couldn't resist. After taking one last look around, I hopped out onto the dock. I waited until I was just past him before I spoke.

"Oh, just a little fire," I said casually.

"Fire!" he said, nearly choking on his plug.

"Yeah. Thought we were going to run her aground at one point, but we got things straightened out."

I paid for the emptied extinguishers—as well as the cost of cleaning the powder residue in the cracks of the deck.

We debated about spending the night in Destin, but decided it was best we hit the road toward Tennessee. Around 8:30 we crossed the Georgia state line. Shortly, our Suburban was filled with the sound of snoring. My crew was exhausted. But somehow I was pretty fresh. In fact, I was experiencing something of an emotional high as I watched the sky turn red at sunset and slip into night.

But as I recalled the just-ended sailing trip and

considered my volatile behavior throughout it, a peculiar notion kept entering my mind: In many ways, I had acted like the obsessed, tyrannical Captain Ahab in *Moby Dick,* about whom I had read in high school. No amount of urgency in any of our situations had warranted the angry commands and criticisms I let fly.

The comparison of myself to Captain Ahab was uncanny and sobering, but also amusing. It struck me that we even shared a common physical trait: gray streaks that ran through the front of our hair!

I considered what I must do to patch things up. First, as soon as Carey was resettled back at college, I would write her a formal letter of apology, explaining in more detail the underlying reasons for my explosive behavior. I would ask her to share it with Chris.

Second, I would propose that we do bareboating again, only this time in the cool of the fall or spring and on a larger sailboat. In the Virgin Islands even!

They'll love it, I thought excitedly. *Why wait? I'll ask everyone now.*

"Hey," I said, leaning back in my seat. "How'd you guys like to do this again in the Virgin Islands at a time when it's cooler? Now that would be the way to go."

For a few moments there was total silence. I wondered if they'd heard me. Then David raised up off the seat where he lay.

"No way, José," he croaked. "You gotta be kiddin'."

➡ *Put on all of God's armor so that you will be able to stand safe against all strategies and tricks of Satan* (Eph. 6:11, TLB).

➡ *Temptation is the stuff of which Christians are made. If the devil never tempts you, you can't develop your resistance to sin* (Billy Sunday).

CHAPTER

MISSION IN SCANDINAVIA

Our plane had long since crossed over Greenland and made its turn toward Scandinavia, where a line of speaking engagements awaited me. We were four hours into our transatlantic flight with three more to go until we landed in Gothenburg, Sweden. Pat, David, and Dale were napping, peacefully oblivious to the pockets of turbulence our plane was encountering over the North Atlantic. Uninterested in sleep, I occupied myself with a magazine.

I had read each sentence an average of three times during the last ten minutes because of the rough dips and jolts our plane was experiencing.

An especially violent drop startled Pat awake.

"Wow!" she said, blinking her eyes rapidly. "What's going on?"

"Turbulence," I said dryly. "I might as well forget reading."

I noticed Pat was studying me. "Have you been asleep?" she asked.

"No, I can't sleep."

"You're not nervous, are you, Ross?"

"No, why?" I replied.

"You just seem a little edgy."

"Ah, well, I do have some butterflies, come to think of it. I just want everything to go well."

She gently squeezed my arm as the plane made another plunge. "It will," she said. "You've got a real purpose in doing this. It's gonna be great."

Giving some thought to Pat's observations about my seeming edginess, I discovered I did, in fact, have some fears about our upcoming days in Sweden and Finland. Foremost in my mind was the fear that we'd encounter difficulty in trying to meet up with our American missionary hosts, Ron and Carol Soderquist, who had organized our itinerary of speaking engagements in Sweden. All we knew about them was that they were blond Americans, which wasn't going to give us a lot to go on in an airport terminal filled with Scandinavians.

Second, I was nagged by doubts of how my messages would be received in Sweden and later in Finland. I'd never before addressed a foreign audience on child-rearing or any other topic. Using a translator would most definitely be a new experience.

To my surprise, the Soderquists had written that news of my coming was being greeted with the enthusiasm afforded a celebrity. Just being in Sweden and Finland as a guest of Sweden for Christ and the Finnish Peoples' Bible Society, respectively, would be thrilling enough. But a celebrity? Me? It was almost too much to take.

I was also very gratified to learn through correspondence with my Finnish publisher that my 1979 book, *How to Really Love Your Child,* had become its number one best-seller in Finland. The Norwegian translation of the book was climbing sales lists in Sweden, thanks in part to the efforts of the Soderquists. This led to the book's being translated into Swedish.

The American couple, working in Sweden under the auspices of Campus Crusade for Christ, had been using the book in Bible study groups in Gothenburg. Carol first employed the book, which at the time was available only in Norwegian, in a Bible study group consisting of young mothers. When the book's final chapter, "Helping Your Child Spiritually," proved an excellent vehicle for witnessing, the couple became very excited and initiated efforts to have the book translated into Swedish.

From our correspondence and telephone conversations, I'd become convinced that the couple was keenly intelligent and committed in a marvelous way to their mission work. Noting the added benefit of their Swedish descent, I saw no reason why the Soderquists should be hindered from achieving their goal of a meaningful Christian revival in Sweden.

The plane's touchdown shortly before 6:00 A.M. interrupted my thoughts and sent us scurrying to collect our personal belongings from overhead and under our seats. I still didn't know how our host was going to locate us in the terminal area. From my window, it appeared the place was alive with early Sunday morning travelers.

As we stepped off the ramp into the gate area, we noticed a tall, blond man neatly dressed in a suit and tie waving wildly at us.

"Ross! Over here," Ron yelled.

We walked quickly toward him. "How did you know it was us?" I asked, putting down my carryon bags to shake his hand.

"From your picture—you know, the picture on the back of your book," he answered.

"Oh, of course," I said, laughing. "What would you have done if I'd grown a beard?"

"It wouldn't have been that difficult," he said. "How

many men do you see around here with dark beards?"

I looked around and smiled. "I see your point."

We collected our luggage and the five of us squeezed into Ron's compact station wagon. He was anxious to show us around his adopted country. During the thirty-minute trip to his home from the airport, he pointed to sights of interest and the beautiful architecture his American family had grown to cherish as much as the natives.

"We'll be leaving for church shortly," Ron said, as he wheeled the car into the driveway of the housing complex where his family lived. "But I know you're all eager to go right to bed."

I agreed. All of us would need our rest for the whirlwind agenda planned for us in the next eight days.

Ron's pretty wife came bounding out of the kitchen to greet us, followed by the Soderquist children—Peter, Anna, and Ingrid.

"We're so glad to finally meet you," Carol said, beaming. She graciously expressed how much my book had meant to her and Ron, as well as to the Swedish parents with whom they'd shared it.

I put up my hands. "Stop," I chuckled, "you'll give me a swelled head."

The four of us took two of the children's rooms and tried to put aside our excitement and get some sleep. We were up by the time our hosts arrived back from church around 12:30. After lunch, we sat around in the living room and discussed our itinerary.

Over the meal, I'd expressed some of my reservations about how my remarks, especially my jokes, would be received by the Swedish people through a translator.

"Being accepted as an author when the book has been published in the language of a particular country is one thing," I said. "But going over as a speaker who doesn't speak the language is another."

"You haven't got a thing to be concerned about, Ross,"

Carol said. "The person we have lined up to serve as your translator is excellent. I promise you nothing will be lost in the translation. Just be yourself."

"Yeah, Ross," Ron piped. "They're gonna love you here. They're gonna really love you. Sweden is ready to welcome you with open arms."

I would have the opportunity shortly to find out just how true their assurances were, as I was due to speak at a church that evening.

Both my fatigue from jet lag and my feelings of uncertainty vanished minutes into my talk. As the Soderquists had promised, the response of the Swedish people to my message was tremendous. I was genuinely overwhelmed by the Christian love expressed by the Gothenburg people.

It had been arranged for me to meet on Monday with the Campus Crusade for Christ staff, which proved to be a wonderful experience. I was uplifted by the commitment of the staff—comprised of Swedish, Finnish, Norwegian, and American workers—to share in bold terms the message of God's love.

Indeed, at each stop on my agenda, a warm feeling was kindled in me as I enjoyed the fellowship of these Christians.

Despite obvious cultural barriers, I felt at one with these believers. Our cross-cultural exchange made me realize the breadth of the work of the Holy Spirit, who can make brothers and sisters out of total strangers from diverse and distant lands.

Ron and Carol had breakfast waiting for us when we awoke Tuesday morning, the day of our move to Stockholm. They were anxious to accompany us on the four-hour train trip to the city and glean our impressions of our first days in Sweden.

After our morning meal, the six of us squeezed once again into Ron's car and headed for the train station. In a short time we were settled in our private train compartment. The conversation quickly gravitated to how successfully my talks had appeared to go over in Gothenburg.

"I'm glad they're getting my message through the translation," I said. "It's just amazing how hungry parents are to hear the benefits of unconditionally loving their children."

Ron remarked that a law passed recently in Sweden prohibited the use of corporal punishment in the discipline of children. The unusual statute, he explained, makes it unlawful not only for parents to spank their children, but to raise their voice or be harsh with them in any way.

"According to the publishers," he pointed out, "your book is one of few American books that approaches childrearing from a non-punitive approach, the only one that emphasizes relating to children through loving techniques."

"Thank you, Ron," I said. "That's good to hear."

"It sounds like there's been a high incidence of child abuse here," Pat interjected. "Is that the reason for the law?"

"Exactly," he replied. "But I don't think child abuse is any more of a problem here than it is in any other country."

We spent a good part of the next hour going through a newspaper Ron had purchased, letting our hosts translate articles of interest for us. Pat and I were intrigued to see how much news from the United States dominated the publication, especially reports of arms buildups and nuclear proliferation. American policies were not cast in the best light, but the Russians fared much worse.

"There's definitely not a lot of love lost between the Scandinavian people and the Russians," Carol said.

"Yeah," Ron chipped in, "we live close enough to see them for what they are."

I suddenly realized we'd heard nothing out of the boys

in quite some time. I glanced up from the paper to find David and Dale with their noses pressed against the window, drinking in every bit of the dramatic, early morning landscape. I was glad to see they were enjoying themselves.

I shared their sense of enjoyment. The rhythmic click-clacking of the rails and the rural scenes of a foreign world had a mesmerizing effect on me. The train trip to Stockholm provided a much-needed repose from our hectic schedule, as well as an excellent opportunity to visit with our hosts.

Our contact upon arriving in the Stockholm train station was Enar Olsson, a representative of Dagen, the Swedish publisher of my book. He must have studied the picture on the book, too, as he spotted us right away.

"Welcome," he said cheerfully. "We're very glad to meet you finally. The people here are very anxious to hear what you have to say."

"Thank you," I replied. "I hope there won't be any problem understanding what I have to say."

"Oh, we have an excellent translator for you," he said. "You're in good hands."

Enar managed to load all of our luggage into his compact car, and then turned to us with a shrug. "I don't have any room for passengers."

"That's OK, Enar," Ron said. "I know the way to the hotel. It's not far. We'll meet you there."

The first thing we noticed after leaving the train station was how much busier Stockholm was than Gothenburg. Its frenetic flow of traffic, typical for a major city, slowed our passage across the street.

Several blocks from the hotel, we noticed a sizable crowd gathered on the sidewalk. A man was gesturing wildly and shouting from atop a wooden box in the center of the gathering. Farther down the same sidewalk, a loudspeaker broadcast more shouted words and music to a smaller crowd.

"Politics," Ron said with a sigh. "We're having national elections, you know."

Enar was waiting for us when we arrived at our hotel. The Tuesday afternoon traffic kept him from beating us by much.

After unloading our luggage, Enar informed us he'd return to drive us to the meeting at seven o'clock. Leaving us in the care of Ron and Carol, he squeezed back into the midday rush of cars and buses.

After we had checked in and eaten a meal at the hotel, Ron and Carol escorted us back out into the lively city of Stockholm. It felt good to get out and stretch our legs and feel the cool, late summer breeze in our faces.

We were taken by the city's charm and cleanliness. From a distance we saw the palace home of the king and queen of Sweden and, at Stockholm Cathedral, further trappings of royalty; the new infant of the royal couple had just been christened there. Military guards arrayed in dazzling dress uniforms and a line of sleek limousines lent a regal air to the mundane street surroundings.

"Perhaps they'll want to read your book," Ron suggested kiddingly. "Even kings need help with their children."

By late afternoon we were back at the hotel. I barely had a chance to flop on the bed and catch my breath before having to get ready for my address at the church. Pat and the boys, exhausted from all the travel, begged off from going with me. I didn't blame them; I was practically seeing double from fatigue.

At 7:00 P.M., Enar appeared in the lobby to pick up Ron, Carol, and myself.

"We'd better hurry," he said. "They're anticipating a large audience."

I felt the butterflies flare up in my stomach. I tried to reassure myself and run over in my head the condensed version of my standard series on children and teenagers.

A large throng of people had, in fact, already amassed

in front of the church's large wooden doors when we arrived.

Enar took us around the back and dropped us off. He'd informed us on the way that he would not be accompanying us due to another pressing engagement. He stuck his head out of the window after I closed the door. "Good luck," he said. "I'll see you tomorrow."

We entered the church through a rear door and were quickly greeted by the church pastor, the associate pastor, and my Swedish interpreter.

"So you're my mouth tonight," I joked to the interpreter.

"Yes," he said, laughing. "Just speak nice and slowly."

"Well, you may have to be my mind, too," I said. "If I should tell a joke or use a humorous expression, make me funny, OK?"

He grinned. "I'll make you funnier than you've ever been."

The address couldn't have gone better. The large audience laughed when it was supposed to laugh and listened intently throughout my talk.

After several minutes in private consultation with the associate pastor, I was ushered into a large room in the church, where a reception in my honor was to be held. Ron and Carol had already disappeared into the gathering of people.

"You look tired," the church official said. "I promise we won't keep you long. There are so many people who want to meet you and ask you questions, but your rest comes first."

The associate pastor excused himself to greet some other guests. I wondered, standing alone in the center of the floor, where all the people were who wanted to speak with me.

Then out of the corner of my eye, I saw a large figure rush toward me. I flinched slightly in reaction to the sudden movement. A large, muscular woman stood before me, her face red with anger. In her right hand she waved a crumpled newspaper.

She suddenly began shouting at me, occasionally slapping my folded arms with her paper. I could only decipher snatches of her agitated yammer, which was delivered in very broken English. What was unequivocally clear, however, was that somehow I had made her very, very upset.

It sounded as if she was condemning the United States for the world's evils—namely sex crimes and nuclear arms, of all things—and holding me personally responsible!

I was absolutely dumbfounded. With each string of verbal assaults, she crowded her burly form closer to mine. Spittle from her mouth landed on my nose and cheeks. When the woman still showed no sign of letting up after another minute, I began to panic. I looked frantically for some assistance, but the people around me were cowering with embarrassment!

Listening to the woman was my only option. By now she had opened the newspaper, which bore the printed image of Lenin in one corner, and pointed to a particular article.

"You country is fault for nuclear arms race!" she screamed. "You make my country bad because we must do the same! Why you come here? Why you lie to these people?"

She had begun looking suspiciously around the room, her eyes darting from one side of the spacious hall to the other. I bent down slightly, nodding my head desperately in mock agreement and trying to look interested in the foreign paper. I prayed she wasn't looking for reinforcements.

I scanned the room myself, hoping to catch sight of the pastor, associate pastor, or my interpreter. When I turned back toward the woman, a terrific force slammed into my stomach!

I doubled over in pain, grabbing the region just below my solar plexus, and dropped to one knee. As I sank down, I let out a loud groan.

Struggling to recapture the breath that had been knocked out of me, I looked at my hands for blood. I thought surely I'd been shot or stabbed. But to my relief there were no wounds.

When I was able to get to my feet, I could see all these Swedes standing around me with puzzled looks on their faces. Few people had actually seen the woman hit me, I reckoned woozily, because she had been standing so close to me when she delivered the blow.

The woman, her fist still clenched and her face contorted in rage, stood just to one side.

In a moment, I was breathing normally and had straightened up completely. I kept my hands up around my midsection to ward off any further shots.

To my horror, the moment I stood upright the woman recommenced her abusive tirade. I fantasized about having a tranquilizer gun.

I needed a new approach. Having gained my composure, I began nodding affirmatively and smiled as sweetly as my shock and pain would allow me.

"Yes, sex crimes are wrong. Yes, nuclear arms are terrible," I said. I promised her that when I got back to the United States I would do everything I could to work against both.

"I'll talk to the people in charge of sex crimes and nuclear arms as soon as I get back," I reassured her. "I'll see that something is done."

My fast-talking fortunately took the wind out of her sails, but I wasn't going to risk another punch to the body. I put one arm around the back of her shoulder and invited her to join me for punch and cookies.

"OK," she said cautiously.

Now that this female time bomb had been disarmed, the Swedes decided it was time to act. A group of men and women surrounded her and pulled her to one side when we reached the reception table. For ten minutes or more, the group appeared to reprimand the woman for her behavior.

When the discussion was over, the woman left the gathering and walked back toward me. I thought momentarily about arming myself with the punch ladle.

"Dr. Campbell," she said formally. "I really must be going now."

"Fine," I said with a sick smile. "Nice seeing you."

After the woman had left, the Swedish people descended on me and offered their sincere apologies. I graciously accepted them, repeatedly dropping the hint that I needed to go to bed.

"I'm so sorry this happened, Dr. Campbell," the associate pastor said on our way outside to catch my cab. "A lot of emotion has been created by the political demonstrations this week. I know you've seen the crowds and heard the loudspeakers."

"Yes, I have," I said. "It's all right. I'm OK now." I smiled as I shook his hand. "Politics have a way of bringing out the worst in us."

Pat was reading and the boys were playing a game when I arrived back at the room.

"Well, how did it go?" Pat asked eagerly. "Did you have a big crowd?"

I grimaced. "Oh, it went great, except for the big Communist woman who punched me in the stomach."

"What?" the three exclaimed in unison. "What in the world happened?" Pat asked.

"Some woman was blaming me for sex crimes and the arms race. She said the Americans were responsible for everything that's wrong in Sweden and the rest of the world."

"That's ridiculous!" Pat said. "Are you OK?"

"Did ya punch her back, Dad?" David asked, drawing back his fist. "Boy, I would have. If some Commie touches me, he's dead meat."

"No, David," I said, sitting down on the bed to remove my shoes. "I didn't punch her back. I barely had enough strength to reason with her."

"Well, I'm sure you did the right thing," Pat said. "We're going to have to be careful."

"Those Commies are the ones who had better be careful," David said, throwing a playful punch at Dale.

"David, we have to watch ourselves," I remarked solemnly. "We're strangers in a strange country. We're at a disadvantage. It's not a game, either."

I explained to them the intolerance with which the Soviet government viewed the Christian faith; it would like nothing better than to orchestrate the annihilation of the church's influence in its country, as well as in bordering nations.

The next day in Stockholm went by without a hitch. The crowds were large and favorably responsive at the state churches where I appeared.

More and more, when our family was alone, we talked about politics and the prevalence of outward Communist influences in Sweden. I was sorry to see the boys had been pulled into the controversial aspects of the trip, and were experiencing anger and fear as a result.

On the final day of our visit in Stockholm, we decided to do some last-minute sightseeing. Ron had joined us in the lobby of our Salvation Army hotel, which was uncharacteristically luxurious for anything bearing the name Salvation Army. Our family would be leaving shortly for the ocean liner that would carry us across the Baltic Sea to Finland.

All of us were eager to look for souvenirs and browse in the shops across the street from our hotel before we left—all of us, that is, except David, who was suffering from an upset stomach.

When Pat suggested we look around a nearby fish market, David plopped down in a chair in the lobby of our hotel.

"Count me out," he said. "I'm sick."

He informed us he would wait for us in the lobby.

After we'd gone, David felt steadily worse and left his chair, opting to stretch out on one of the exquisitely upholstered couches along a wall in the hotel lobby.

In any American hotel, it's doubtful that such an act would create a big stir. Due to his illness, however, David forgot he was not in his homeland.

The manager apparently saw David asleep on the couch, and, mistaking him for a bum of some kind, summoned the hotel's bouncers. As David tells the story, the two men seized him by the shoulder and proceeded to escort him to the front door. His protests in English failed to persuade the men that he was "not causing any trouble."

Fortunately, Carol happened to be walking into the lobby at the time. She squealed in alarm. She told the men that David was not a young drunk off the street, as they suspected, but an American guest of the hotel.

"Tell 'em I'm sick!" David shouted. "Tell 'em I'm sick!"

When we returned to hear David's woeful tale, all of us had a hard time stifling our laughter.

Dale was practically in stitches.

"You're the first person I know to get thrown out of a Salvation Army hotel," he roared.

In our cabin on the boat to Finland, I managed to talk to David alone. I felt the time was perfect to make several points that might help him understand the events of the last few days.

"They kind of roughed us up back there, didn't they?" I asked.

"Yeah, they did," he said. "They don't like Americans very much, do they?"

It was obvious our experiences in Scandinavia had given David a real education in international affairs. The political tensions he'd heard and read about in the news had become real matters for consideration.

"It's not so much that they don't like Americans," I said. "It's just that friction builds up when people misunderstand or misinterpret the intentions of one another. An absence of communication is the reason for that."

I drew a parallel between being an outsider in a foreign country and being a Christian in an unchristian world.

"Even when you have the best intentions, people will try to hurt you. Some people," I added, "are wrongly conditioned to get you, like that Communist woman. And some people are out to get you just for the sake of getting you.

"The world is filled with indifference and hatred," I added.

"I understand why we're over here now," he said. "I see why it's important for you to do what you're doing. People have to stand up for things. You have to let people know where you're at."

I looked at David with admiration and nodded. "Yes, that's right. We can't be afraid to speak up if our words can help someone. Jesus certainly wasn't."

"But sometimes speaking up gets you into trouble," he observed. "I mean, somebody could have just wiped you out back there—like that woman."

I nodded thoughtfully. "Jesus spoke up," I said, "and was crucified for it."

"Turning the other cheek when people are mean is hard, isn't it?" David asked quietly. "Especially when someone tries to hurt you and you know you're doing what's right."

I thought for a moment. "Yeah," I replied, "it's hard sometimes not to lash out. You've got to keep your perspective.

"It's really hard," I added, chuckling, "when a woman twice your size is standing over you and daring you to get up."

➧ *But I say to you, do not resist him who is evil; but whoever slaps you on your right cheek, turn to him the other also. . . .*

You have heard that it was said, "You shall love your neighbor, and hate your enemy."

But I say to you, love your enemies, and pray for those who persecute you in order that you may be sons of your Father who is in heaven. . . . (Matt. 5:39, 43-45, NASB).

➧ *Love is a gift, take it, let it grow.*
Love is a sign we should wear, let it show.
Love is an act, do it, let it go (William Penn).

EPILOGUE

I hope no one believes that my desire to share my stories and insights suggests that I have arrived. Maintaining spiritual perspective in the face of life's storms is an ongoing challenge for me. Like everyone else, I'm continually growing emotionally and spiritually, trying not to look behind, but always "pressing toward the mark" (Phil. 3:14).

For each of us, real inner growth depends upon our willingness to trust in a God who deeply loves us and has a wonderful plan for each of us. Hardships do not mean he cares for us any less. The fact that we stumble and fall is a demonstration of God's desire not to make us mindless robots. If we were robots or pawns created solely for his pleasure, the bond we've been granted with him through Christ would be meaningless.

Dredging up my vulnerabilities and heartaches for

publication has been a sobering exercise. Focusing on the hard times, however, has pointed me to God's wondrous grace—grace that has enabled our family tree to weather all the storms intact.

For the record, here's where the Campbell family is now.

In addition to practicing psychiatry in Chattanooga, I've had numerous occasions to travel across the country and speak to church congregations and other groups on the critical issues of childrearing and child development. When my schedule hasn't permitted me to accept speaking engagements, we've been able to suggest a new four-part film series based on my second book, *How to Really Love Your Teenager*, to fill the need.

Pat, whose steady perspective on life and faith continues to be an inspiration to me, spends the better part of her days seeing that our boys—David, now seventeen, and Dale, now thirteen—have clean football, basketball, and baseball uniforms and a sufficient amount of food to satisfy their ravenous appetites. Mind you, the boys don't have every whim—especially the extravagant ones—catered to, but with David now having at least an inch and several pounds on me, I give extra consideration to his requests.

As for Carey and Chris, whom you intimately met in "The Great Family Sailing Disaster," they live slightly more than a mile from us (to our great delight) in their new home on Signal Mountain. Carey currently works at a Chattanooga hospital as an outpatient surgical assistant and Chris is employed by a local law firm.

And now for Cathy.

One question we didn't anticipate after the release of my first book, *How to Really Love Your Child*, but which we frequently received, pertained to the whereabouts of our daughter Cathy, who was not shown in the family picture on the book's back cover. We quickly alerted the publisher to the interest that had been raised by Cathy's absence from the picture, and a clarification was printed on subsequent covers.

Cathy, now twenty-three, still resides at the Sunland Center for Retarded Children in Marrianna, Florida. She has only recently learned to walk unassisted. To this day, Cathy requires help in eating and getting dressed. Mentally, she has not progressed beyond six months.

Cathy's days are not filled with what most of us would call normal routines, obviously. But we believe Cathy is happy. Although she is unable to recognize any of us during our visits with her, she has a family who loves her very much. And, despite her impaired faculties, we know that she is also a member of God's family and will share in all the joys of eternal life with the Father.

To all of you who have expressed interest in Cathy, we say thank you. To you who are parents of children with handicaps or disabilities, we ask that God's richest blessings and offerings of peace will be upon you.

"Why?" is a question that crosses the lips of every parent whose child is seriously afflicted in some way. There are no easy answers, but we believe the Lord feels the grief and pain of these parents just as intensely as they do.

Fortunately, with his grace and the example and support of mature Christians who have walked the same difficult road, spiritual perspective is possible. This is my prayer for you.